HELLFIRE

THE FLAMES THAT TRANSFORM

Tina Ketch

HELLFIRE
THE FLAMES THAT TRANSFORM

ISBN: 979-8-9923083-2-7
eISBN: 979-8-9923083-3-4

First Printing, 2025

For additional resources, insights, and updates from Tina Ketch, visit **TinaKetch.com** or follow her on social media.

TinaKetch@me.com

DEDICATION

To the brave souls who dare to step into the fire, This book is for you.

To those who have felt the searing heat of pain, loss, doubt, or fear, who have stood at the edge of their breaking point and wondered if they could endure—This is your testament: you are stronger than you know.

To the seekers, the healers, the dreamers, and the fighters, to those who refuse to let the flames define them but choose instead to be refined by them—This is your reminder: the light you seek is already within you.

To the quiet moments when you rise, scarred but unbroken, to the fierce courage it takes to face your shadows, and to the radiant beauty that emerges when you embrace your truth—This is your celebration: the fire transforms, but it cannot destroy.

And to the light—yours, mine, and ours—that illuminates even the darkest nights, that reveals our strength, our resilience, and our boundless capacity to grow, this is your tribute: a life touched by fire is a life touched by grace.

May these pages be a companion on your journey, a guide as you navigate the flames, and a beacon to remind you that the fire, no matter how fierce, always carries the promise of transformation.

With gratitude for your courage and the light that will transform your life, this book is dedicated to you.

PREFACE

There is a fire that burns within all of us—a fire that can consume, devastate, and leave us feeling as though we are standing in the ruins of our own lives. This fire is often misunderstood, feared, and avoided at all costs. We call it by many names: pain, loss, grief, failure, guilt, anger. But I call it Hellfire.

Hellfire is not a punishment, though it often feels like one. It is not something inflicted upon us to destroy us, though its flames may reduce us to our most vulnerable state. Hellfire is, in its essence, a force of transformation. The fire burns away illusions, clears the path of what no longer serves us, and leaves us standing in the raw truth of who we are. It is a crucible; within its flames, we are forged into something more substantial, purer, and authentic.

This book was born from recognizing that Hellfire is an inevitable part of life. We all walk through it at some point—whether through the torment of mental anguish, the ache of a grieving heart, the toll of physical suffering, the crisis of faith, or the overwhelming energy of psychic storms. And yet, as much as we resist it, this fire also holds a profound gift. It teaches us lessons that cannot be learned in comfort. It reveals strengths we did not know we possessed. It shapes us, not by sparing us from pain but by guiding us through it.

As I explored the concept of Hellfire more deeply, I realized that it is not a singular experience but a multi-faceted phenomenon. It is mental when our minds are consumed by self-doubt, overthinking, or fear. It is physical when our bodies carry the weight of stress, illness, or neglect. It is emotional when our hearts are burdened with grief, anger, or unspoken truths. It is spiritual when we feel abandoned by the divine or disconnected from our purpose. And it is psychic when heightened intuition or energetic sensitivity leaves us feeling unmoored. Each dimension of Hellfire is unique, yet they are all interconnected, weaving together to create the tapestry of our trials.

In this book, I invite you to journey through these dimensions of Hellfire—not as a bystander but as an active participant in your transformation. You will meet individuals who have faced their fires, their stories offering a mirror for your experiences. Through their struggles, you will see the universal nature of Hellfire, and through their triumphs, you will find hope. These stories are not about avoiding or extinguishing the fire but embracing it, walking through it, and emerging renewed.

I do not offer a prescription for avoiding pain—because to live is to experience pain. Instead, I offer tools, reflections, and practices for navigating it. From reframing our mental narratives to fostering emotional resilience, from creating environments that support growth to cultivating spiritual and psychic grounding, this book provides a roadmap for transforming Hellfire into light.

But this is not just a book about surviving—it is about thriving. Hellfire does not only burn; it also illuminates. It reveals the truth of who we are, the depth of our strength, and the breadth of our potential. It challenges us to look at the parts of ourselves we may have hidden away, confront the fears we have avoided, and embrace the growth that comes from struggle.

Writing this book has been a journey through my Hellfires. It has required me to revisit the moments that broke me, the trials that reshaped me, and the lessons I continue to learn. It has reminded me that Hellfire is not something we pass through once but encounter throughout our lives, each time emerging with a deeper understanding of ourselves and the world.

I hope the pages will serve as a companion on your journey. You will find comfort in knowing you are not alone, strength in seeing the resilience of others, and guidance in the practices and insights shared. Most of all, I hope you will see the fire not as something to fear but as something to embrace—a force that, though fierce, can transform.

We cannot avoid the flames, but we can walk through them. We can let them shape us, not into ashes, but into something radiant, something whole. This is the gift of Hellfire. It does not leave us where it found us. It carries us forward, burning away the old to make way for the new.

Welcome to Hellfire: The Flames That Transform. May you find courage in the fire and light in its glow.

TABLE OF CONTENTS

INTRODUCTION TO HELLFIRE

THE FLAMES THAT TRANSFORM

Hellfire. The word itself evokes an immediate reaction—an image of raging flames, consuming and relentless, a force feared for its destructive power. It has long been associated with the ultimate punishment, a symbol of torment and suffering, divine wrath, and eternal damnation. But what if we looked at Hellfire through a different lens? What if its flames, rather than annihilating, were purifying? What if they held the seeds of transformation, resilience, and renewal within them?

In every life, Hellfire manifests in some form. It may come as the anguish of loss, the torment of guilt, the searing pain of failure, or the relentless trials of a soul searching for meaning. These flames are not confined to any sphere of existence—they burn through our minds, bodies, emotions, and spirits, leaving no part of us untouched. Yet, as much as we may fear them, these fires are also essential. They strip away illusions, confront us with our most profound truths, and forge within us a new strength.

This book is not a tale of destruction but one of transformation. It explores the many faces of Hellfire as they appear in our modern lives—through mental anguish, emotional turmoil, physical suffering, spiritual crises, and the psychic storms of heightened intuition and energy. It delves into how we encounter these fires, the challenges they bring, and the profound lessons they offer when we dare to walk through them.

You will meet individuals who have faced their own Hellfire: the single parent overwhelmed by guilt yet discovering joy in the smallest moments; the professional consumed by burnout but finding purpose anew; the grieving spouse who transforms sorrow into a source of strength; the spiritual seeker lost in doubt who rekindles their connection to the divine. These stories, though deeply personal, are universal. They reflect the trials we all face and the resilience we all possess.

This book is not only about understanding Hellfire but about transforming it. It provides practical tools for fostering resilience, shifting perspectives, and creating environments that support growth and healing. It challenges you to see the fire not as your enemy but as your teacher—a force that can refine and illuminate, even as it tests you.

Whether you are facing a storm in your relationships, career, health, or spiritual path, this book invites you to step into the flames with courage. Here, in the heart of the fire, we find not destruction but rebirth. Hellfire may scorch and test us, but it reveals our strength, truth, and light.

Let this guide you as you walk through the fire, emerging not as ashes but as something renewed, whole, and radiant. For in every flame, there is the power not only to burn but also to transform.

Welcome to Hellfire: The Flames That Transform. May these pages light your way.

WHY READ HELLFIRE

THE FLAMES THAT TRANSFORM WILL ELEVATE YOUR LIFE

This book is not just a collection of stories, insights, and practices but a guide to transformation. Life's trials are inevitable, and the flames of Hellfire will touch every soul at some point. What sets the path forward is not whether we encounter the fire but how we respond to it. Hellfire: The Flames That Transform offers you the tools, wisdom, and inspiration to endure life's challenges and thrive because of them.

Here's why reading this book will elevate your life:

1. It Will Change Your Perspective on Pain
   Pain, struggle, and hardship are often considered enemies to avoid or conquer. This book reframes these experiences as necessary elements of growth. By understanding Hellfire as a force of transformation rather than destruction, you will learn to embrace your struggles as opportunities for renewal. It will help you see that your darkest moments are not the end but the beginning of a more profound, meaningful journey.
2. It Will Teach You Resilience
   Through real-life stories and practical guidance, this book demonstrates how to navigate life's toughest challenges with strength and grace. It offers tools to develop mental, emotional, physical, and spiritual resilience, empowering you to rise from the ashes of adversity more potent than ever. These lessons are not just theoretical—they are actionable, providing you with strategies you can implement daily.
3. It Will Deepen Your Self-Awareness
   The flames of Hellfire reveal the hidden parts of ourselves—the fears we avoid, the beliefs we cling to, and the strengths we underestimate. This book will guide you in uncovering these truths, helping you understand who you are and what truly matters

to you. With this awareness, you will be better equipped to make choices aligned with your values and purpose.

4. It Will Rekindle Your Connection to the Divine
   Whether you define the divine as a higher power, the interconnectedness of all things, or the spark of light within yourself, this book will help you reconnect with that sacred energy. It explores the spiritual dimension of Hellfire, offering insights and practices to find meaning, purpose, and peace even amid life's most incredible storms.
5. It Will Help You Build a Life of Light
   Hellfire: The Flames That Transform is not about surviving but thriving. It is a call to action to live fully and authentically, to use the lessons of the fire to illuminate your path forward. When you close this book, you will have a renewed sense of hope, a clearer vision for your life, and the tools to create a future filled with light, meaning, and joy.
6. It Will Connect You to a Universal Truth
   The experiences of Hellfire—loss, grief, doubt, and transformation—are universal. This book reminds you that you are not alone in your journey. Through its stories and reflections, you will see yourself and others in yourself. It will foster a connection to the shared human experience and inspire you to contribute your light to the world.

The Promise of Transformation

By reading this book, you choose to face the fire with courage. You are choosing to transform rather than be consumed, to grow rather than remain stagnant, and to emerge from the flames as a more resilient, empowered, and radiant version of yourself.

This book is your companion on that journey—a guide, a teacher, and a mirror to your strength. It will elevate your life because it will show you that the fire you feared holds the light you've been seeking all along.

COMMON USES OF "HELLFIRE" IN MODERN TIMES

1. **Religious and Theological Contexts**

   - **Traditional Usage:**

   In Christian theology, particularly among evangelical or fundamentalist groups, "Hellfire" is still used to describe divine judgment and the eternal torment of sinners.

   Hellfire sermons or teachings invoke vivid imagery of fire as a metaphor for punishment, urging repentance and spiritual commitment.

   - **Example:**

   "The preacher delivered a fiery sermon about the dangers of sin and the reality of Hellfire."

2. **Metaphor for Intense Emotional or Physical Pain**

   - **Common Meaning:**

   Hellfire is often used metaphorically to describe situations of extreme distress, emotional torment, or intense challenges.

   It can refer to feelings like guilt, shame, anger, or even physical suffering such as burning pain.

   - **Example:**

   "Her breakup felt like walking through Hellfire, leaving her emotionally scorched."

3. **Symbol of Transformation or Purification**

- **Modern Interpretation:**

Some use Hellfire as a symbol of trials that lead to personal growth, transformation, or purification. This aligns with the idea of "walking through the fire" to emerge stronger or more enlightened.

- **Example:**

"He went through the Hellfire of addiction and recovery, emerging as a better version of himself."

4. **Pop Culture and Media**

- **Usage in Entertainment:**

Hellfire frequently appears as a dramatic or supernatural element in movies, TV shows, books, and games. It often symbolizes evil, destruction, or apocalyptic scenarios.

It is commonly associated with demonic imagery, fantasy worlds, or moral dilemmas.

- **Example:**

Disney's The Hunchback of Notre Dame features a song titled "Hellfire," reflecting inner conflict and temptation.

In video games or fantasy novels, Hellfire is often depicted as a weapon or spell, emphasizing its destructive power.

5. **Colloquial and Hyperbolic Expressions**

- **Everyday Language:**

The term is sometimes used casually or hyperbolically to describe situations of extreme intensity, whether humorous or serious.

It might refer to fiery debates, harsh criticism, or extreme weather conditions.

- **Examples:**

"The boss unleashed Hellfire during the meeting after the project failed."

"The heatwave felt like Hellfire, making the summer unbearable."

6. **Political and Military Terminology**

- **Weaponry:**

"Hellfire" has been adopted as the name of a missile system used by the military, emphasizing its destructive precision and firepower.

- **Example:**

The AGM-114 Hellfire missile is used by the U.S. military, reinforcing the term's association with overwhelming power.

7. **Symbol in Personal or Collective Struggles**

- **Resonance in Self-Help and Transformation:**

In modern self-help or philosophical discussions, Hellfire may symbolize internal struggles like mental health battles, grief, or life's challenges that test one's resilience and character.

- **Example:**

  "To heal from trauma is to walk through your own Hellfire and find peace on the other side."

How "Hellfire" Reflects Contemporary Themes

In modern usage, "Hellfire" reflects a balance between its traditional meanings and its metaphorical expansion:

1. **Intensity:** It often conveys a sense of extreme heat, destruction, or urgency.
2. **Transformation:** It symbolizes trials that purify or reveal more profound truths.
3. **Emotion:** It encapsulates the depth of human experiences, from anguish to catharsis.
4. **Dramatic Flair:** It's used for dramatic effect, emphasizing the seriousness or intensity of a situation.

While "Hellfire" originated as a theological term tied to divine punishment, its modern usage is much broader. It has become a versatile metaphor for intensity, struggle, transformation, and destruction across religion, culture, entertainment, and everyday language. This evolution reflects its enduring power to capture the depth and complexity of human experiences.

MENTAL HELLFIRE: THE INFERNO WITHIN

Definition Recap

Mental Hellfire is the relentless turmoil of the mind, a furnace where doubts, fears, and insecurities rage like unyielding flames. It is a space where thoughts loop endlessly, amplifying anxieties, suffocating hope, and leaving one in internal paralysis. Mental Hellfire is not just a battle but a crucible, where the mind's greatest tormentors reveal themselves and where, if faced courageously, profound transformation can occur.

Short Story: The Unyielding Question

"Am I Enough?"

Evelyn stared at the spreadsheet on her computer screen, her fingers hovering over the keyboard, frozen. The numbers blurred together into an incomprehensible haze. It wasn't the task that overwhelmed her—it was the unrelenting voice in her head, whispering louder and louder as the minutes passed.

"You don't know what you're doing."

"You're going to make a mistake, and they'll all see it."

"Why did they even hire you?"

The whispers were cruel but familiar, like an unwanted companion who had walked beside her for years. The voice never relented no matter how much she achieved—promotion, accolades, or praise from her peers. If anything, it grew louder with every success, as though it were desperate to pull her back into the shadows.

The breaking point came during a team meeting. Evelyn's manager, a pragmatic but well-meaning man, glanced at her report and remarked, "Good start, Evelyn, but let's make sure we don't miss any details." It was a harmless comment meant to encourage refinement, but to Evelyn, it felt like confirmation of her worst fear: I'm not enough.

That night, Evelyn couldn't sleep. She lay awake, staring at the ceiling, her mind spinning. Every mistake she'd ever made replayed in vivid detail—like a highlight reel of failure. The time she'd misspoke during a presentation. The email she'd sent with a typo. The look of disappointment on her manager's face when a project had been delayed, even though it wasn't entirely her fault.

The fire in her mind grew hotter, consuming her thoughts and leaving her restless. Her chest tightened, and a dull ache spread through her stomach. She avoided looking at her partner, Steven, who had tried to comfort her earlier in the evening. "You're too hard on yourself," he'd said. But his words had only made her feel worse. If he knew how broken, he wouldn't say that.

The First Spark of Change

Weeks passed, and Evelyn sank deeper into her Mental Hellfire. She began to withdraw—avoiding friends, canceling plans, and staying late at work to drown out the noise in her head with endless tasks. She told herself it was temporary and needed to push through. But deep down, she knew she was burning out.

While cleaning her closet one Saturday afternoon, Evelyn stumbled upon an old journal. Its leather cover was worn, and the pages were slightly yellowed. She opened it to the first page, where she had written a quote years ago:

"The fire that burns within you is also the fire that can light your way."

The words struck her like a bolt of lightning. She didn't remember where she'd heard them, but they felt significant. Evelyn felt a flicker of curiosity for the first time in weeks—an ember amidst the ashes. She sat down and began to write. At first, the words came hesitantly, haltingly. But soon, the pen seemed to move independently, pouring out her thoughts, fears, and frustrations.

Peering Into the Flames

As Evelyn journaled, patterns began to emerge. She saw how the critical voice in her head wasn't indeed her own. It was the echo of her childhood, where her parents had demanded perfection in everything she did. It was the residue of a workplace culture that equated worth with productivity. It resulted from years spent suppressing her emotions, fearing they would make her appear weak.

She also noticed her voice was loud when she was tired or overwhelmed. The connection was clear: her inner fire thrived on exhaustion and self-neglect. For the first time, Evelyn saw the Hellfire for what it was—a manifestation of her unacknowledged pain and unmet needs.

Transforming the Flames

With this awareness, Evelyn began to make small but deliberate changes. She set boundaries at work, saying no to extra tasks when her plate was full. She practiced mindfulness, taking five minutes each morning to breathe deeply and ground herself. She reached out to a therapist who could help her navigate the depths of her inner world.

At first, the changes felt insignificant, like trying to extinguish a forest fire with a single drop of water. But over time, the fire began to shift. It no longer consumed her. Instead, it became a source of light, illuminating the path forward.

One evening, months later, Evelyn sat with Steven, sharing her journey for the first time. "I've been so afraid," she admitted, tears streaming down her face. "Afraid that I'll never be enough. But I'm starting to see that I may not have to be perfect. Maybe I have to be me."

Steven took her hand, his eyes filled with understanding. "You are more than enough, Evelyn. Always have been."

The Lesson of Mental Hellfire

Evelyn's story shows that Mental Hellfire, though painful, is not an enemy. It is a messenger urging us to confront the thoughts and beliefs that no longer serve us. It reminds us that the potential for profound transformation lies within the flames of doubt and fear.

Key Insights:

1. Awareness Sparks Change: Recognizing the source of the inner fire is the first step to taming it.
2. Small Steps Matter: Setting boundaries, seeking support, and practicing self-compassion are potent tools for navigating Mental Hellfire.
3. Healing is a Journey: The fire doesn't disappear overnight but can become a guiding light with patience and persistence.

PHYSICAL HELLFIRE: THE BODY'S INFERNO

Definition Recap

Physical Hellfire manifests within the body, often as a direct result of prolonged stress, unresolved emotional pain, or the strain of carrying burdens that the mind and heart refuse to release. It is the physical embodiment of internal turmoil—a fiery signal the body sends when it can no longer bear the weight of neglect, tension, or emotional suppression. Unlike fleeting discomfort, this fire burns persistently, demanding attention and transformation.

Short Story: The Body Speaks

Maria stood in the middle of her bustling kitchen, the aroma of garlic and onions sizzling in olive oil filling the air. It was her youngest son's birthday, and the house was alive with laughter and chatter. Her mother-in-law orchestrated the decorations, her husband wrangled the kids, and Maria ensured everything went perfectly.

But as she reached for the next ingredient, a sharp pain shot through her lower back. She froze, gripping the counter to steady herself. It wasn't the first time she'd felt it—this dull, burning ache that seemed to linger just out of reach. She had ignored it for weeks, brushing it off as a sign of aging or poor posture. But today, it felt different. It was angrier, hotter, more insistent.

"Are you okay?" her husband called out, concern flickering.

"I'm fine," Maria replied automatically, forcing a smile. She didn't have time for pain—not today, not ever. There were meals to cook, homework to help with, bills to pay, and expectations to meet. Pain would have to wait.

The Fire Within

Maria's back pain didn't wait. Over the next few weeks, it grew worse, radiating down her legs and making even simple tasks unbearable. She began waking up in the middle of the night, her body stiff and unyielding. The pain crept into her shoulders and neck, manifesting as a constant tightness that no amount of stretching or massaging could relieve.

Her doctor ran tests, ruling out significant injuries or illnesses. "It's likely stress," he suggested gently. "Your muscles are holding tension. Have you thought about taking it easy?"

Maria almost laughed at the suggestion. "Take it easy." How could she? She was the glue that held her family together. If she stopped, everything would fall apart. But deep down, she knew the doctor was right. She wasn't just tired—she was burned out.

One evening, after putting the kids to bed, Maria sat alone in the living room, her heating pad draped across her back. Tears filled her eyes as she stared at the family photo on the mantel. She loved her life, but she felt trapped by it. She was carrying so much—too much—and her body was screaming for relief.

The Breaking Point

The turning point came one morning when Maria tried to lift a basket of laundry and collapsed to the floor, her back seizing in agony. Her husband rushed to her side, his face pale with worry. "Maria, this isn't normal," he said. "You need help."

For the first time, Maria didn't argue. She allowed herself to be vulnerable, admitting how much pain she was in—not just physically but emotionally. She realized that the fire in her body wasn't just about the physical tasks she'd been doing; it was about everything she'd been holding inside: the pressure to be perfect, the fear of letting others down, and the belief that her worth was tied to how much she could accomplish.

The Path to Healing

Maria's journey to extinguish her Physical Hellfire wasn't quick or easy. She began by seeing a physical therapist, who helped her address the tension in her muscles and taught her stretches that released years of built-up stress. But the real breakthrough came when she started journaling—something she hadn't done since high school.

Through writing, Maria uncovered the emotions she had buried beneath her responsibilities. She wrote about her childhood, where she had learned to equate love with self-sacrifice. She wrote about her anger, her sadness, and even her resentment—emotions she had never allowed herself to feel, let alone express.

She also started meditating, something that initially felt foreign and uncomfortable. Sitting quietly with herself was terrifying initially, as it forced her to face the chaos. But over time, the practice became a sanctuary, a space where she could let go of the burdens she had been carrying for so long.

The Flame Transformed

Months later, Maria stood in her kitchen again, cooking another meal for her family. But this time, the atmosphere was different. She wasn't rushing or multitasking; she was present, savoring the process. Her back still twinged occasionally, but the searing, relentless pain was gone.

Maria had learned to say no to extra responsibilities, toxic perfectionism, and the inner voice that told her she had to do it all. She had learned to listen to her body, recognizing that pain wasn't an enemy but a messenger. Her Physical Hellfire had forced her to slow down, reflect, and rebuild her life in a way that honored her well-being.

The Lesson of Physical Hellfire

Maria's story teaches us that Physical Hellfire is the body's way of communicating when words and thoughts have failed. It forces us to confront the imbalance in our lives and invites us to make changes that align with our physical, emotional, and spiritual needs.

Key Insights:

1. Pain Is a Messenger: Physical discomfort often signals deeper emotional or mental struggles that need attention.
2. Balance Is Essential: Overworking and neglecting self-care can ignite Physical Hellfire, but rest mindfulness, and boundaries can extinguish it.
3. Healing Takes Courage: Facing the root cause of physical pain requires vulnerability, patience, and self-compassion.

EMOTIONAL HELLFIRE: THE BURNING HEART

Definition Recap

Emotional Hellfire is the searing pain of intense feelings that overwhelm and consume, leaving one raw and exposed. It manifests as grief, rage, shame, or despair—emotions so powerful they feel like flames engulfing the heart. Emotional Hellfire can be devastating, but it also has the power to cleanse, heal, and transform when faced with courage and authenticity.

Short Story: The Burn of Betrayal

Emma leaned against the kitchen counter, clutching her phone. The message on the screen blurred as tears filled her eyes, but she didn't need to reread it. The words were already seared into her mind. "I never wanted to hurt you, but I can't do this anymore."

It was over. Ten years, countless dreams and plans for the future are gone instantly. Her fiancé, Liam, had walked away without warning, leaving nothing but a text message and the echo of his absence. The betrayal hit her like a punch, leaving her breathless and hollow.

At first, Emma felt nothing but shock. She went through the motions of her day, numb and robotic. But as the hours turned into days, the numbness gave way to something far worse: anger. It was a white-hot, blistering rage that consumed her every thought. She replayed every argument, every moment she had overlooked, every sign she had missed. How could he do this to her? How could he leave without a word?

The anger was relentless, but it was also a mask. Beneath it lay a deep, aching grief—a grief so profound it felt like her heart was being torn apart. Emma cried until no tears were left, only the hollow ache of emptiness. She stopped answering calls, avoided friends, and withdrew into the silence of her apartment. She was alone with the fire, and it was eating her alive.

The Breaking Point

One night, Emma sat on the bathroom floor, clutching an old sweatshirt from Liam. It still smelled faintly of his cologne, and the scent brought back memories—his laugh, the way he'd held her hand, the plans they'd made to travel the world together. The fire inside her erupted, and she screamed into the fabric, a raw, guttural sound that came from the depths of her soul.

At that moment, something shifted. The fire didn't die down, but it changed. It wasn't just anger or grief any more; it was something deeper, something ancient. It was the realization that she wasn't just mourning Liam's betrayal—she was mourning every time she had betrayed herself. Every time, she had silenced her voice to keep the peace. Every time, she had settled for less than she deserved. Every time, she had ignored her own needs to make someone else happy.

The flames burned brighter, but for the first time, Emma didn't fight them. She let them rage, consuming the lies she had told herself and the dreams that no longer served her. She realized the fire wasn't there to destroy her but to transform her.

The Path to Healing

Emma began the slow process of rebuilding. She started therapy, where she learned to face her emotions instead of running from them. Her therapist explained that grief and anger were natural parts of healing, but they were also teachers. The fire had a purpose: to strip away the old and make way for the new.

Emma took out a journal and wrote a letter to Liam one day. She didn't hold back—she poured out her anger, hurt, and disappointment. But as the words flowed, something surprising happened. The anger gave way to gratitude—gratitude for the love they had shared, the lessons she had learned, and even the heartbreak that had forced her to grow.

She didn't send the letter. Instead, she burned it in a small ceremony, watching the flames consume the words. As the ashes scattered, Emma felt a weight lift from her heart. The fire that had once threatened to destroy her now felt like a warm ember, a reminder of her strength and resilience.

THE IMPACT ON OTHERS

Emma's journey through Emotional Hellfire didn't just change her—it changed her relationships. She reconnected with friends she had pushed away, apologizing for her distance and sharing her story. Her vulnerability inspired others to open up about their struggles, creating a more profound sense of connection.

Emma also sets boundaries in her relationships, valuing her needs and desires in a way she has never done before. She realized the fire had taught her to honor herself so she could show up more fully for others.

The Lesson of Emotional Hellfire

Emma's story illustrates that Emotional Hellfire, while painful, is a force of transformation. It forces us to face the depths of our emotions, teaching us to release what no longer serves us and to rebuild with authenticity and strength.

Key Insights:

1. Feel to Heal: Avoiding or suppressing emotions only intensifies the fire. Facing them with honesty and courage allows for proper healing.
2. Transformation Through Pain: Emotional Hellfire strips away illusions, leaving behind only what is fundamental and essential.
3. Strength in Vulnerability: Sharing our pain can deepen connections and inspire others to face their fires.

Psychic Hellfire: The Energetic Storm

Definition Recap

Psychic Hellfire is an overwhelming flood of energetic, intuitive, or otherworldly experiences that challenge one's understanding of reality. It can be triggered by heightened sensitivity to unseen forces, unresolved trauma manifesting psychically, or a sudden spiritual awakening. This form of Hellfire forces individuals to confront the vastness of their own consciousness and the interconnected energies of the universe.

Short Story: The Whispering Shadows

Olivia's journey began with subtle signs of her unique sensitivity. As a child, she could discern the unspoken emotions of those around her with uncanny accuracy. Her mother's hidden sadness, her father's suppressed frustration—these were not mysteries to her. But as she matured, her sensitivity began to intensify in ways she couldn't comprehend.

It started subtly, with dreams that felt more like memories. A woman in a red dress stood at the edge of a forest, calling her name. A shadowy figure handed her a golden key. Olivia would wake up drenched in sweat, her heart pounding. Then came the whispers—soft, indistinct murmurs that seemed to come from nowhere and everywhere at once. At first, she thought she was imagining things, but the whispers grew louder and more insistent until she could no longer ignore them.

The Fire Ignites

One evening, after a particularly vivid dream, Olivia sat in her bedroom, staring at the candle on her desk. The flame danced in the dim light, casting shadows on the walls. As she watched, a sudden chill ran down her spine, and the whispers began again. This time, they were clearer. "Look within," they urged. "The answers are inside."

The words terrified her. She didn't want to look within. She was already overwhelmed by the storm of emotions and sensations that seemed to flood her every waking moment. Her body ached with tension, her mind raced with questions, and her heart felt heavy with an unshakable sadness. She was consumed by Mental Hellfire, her thoughts spiraling out of control. Her chest burned with the unresolved grief of lost loved ones—Emotional Hellfire that she had buried for years. Her body ached under the weight of unspoken truths—Physical Hellfire manifesting in knots of tension and fatigue. And her faith wavered, as she questioned the very nature of reality and her place in it—Spiritual Hellfire raging in the background.

The Breaking Point

Olivia's turning point arrived on a night of desperation. Seeking relief, she found herself in a meditation circle led by a friend. The room was filled with the soothing hum of singing bowls, the air heavy with the scent of sage. Olivia, hesitant but willing to try anything, closed her eyes and sank into the meditation.

As Olivia delved deeper into the meditation, a profound shift occurred. The whispers returned, but this time, they were not frightening—they were familiar. They guided her to a memory she had long buried: standing in her grandmother's garden, surrounded by vibrant flowers and the warmth of the sun. Her grandmother's words echoed in her mind, 'You have a gift, Olivia. It's not a burden—it's a light. But you have to embrace it.'

Tears streamed down Olivia's face as the memory washed over her. She realized that the fire she had been running from wasn't trying to destroy her—it was trying to awaken her. The whispers weren't external—they were her own intuition, urging her to step into her power.

Intertwining the Fires

Over the next few weeks, Olivia began to confront each aspect of her Hellfire:

- Mental: She practiced mindfulness, learning to quiet her racing thoughts and create space for clarity.

- Emotional: She journaled about her grief and fear, allowing herself to feel and release the emotions she had suppressed.
- Physical: She started yoga, using movement to release the tension stored in her body.
- Spiritual: She embraced meditation and prayer, reconnecting with the sense of wonder and purpose she had lost.

Through these practices, Olivia learned to harness her sensitivity rather than fear it. She realized that Psychic Hellfire was the culmination of all the other aspects, a storm of energies that demanded integration and balance. The fire burned away her resistance, leaving her with a profound sense of clarity and connection.

OLIVIA: THE RIPPLE EFFECT

As Olivia embraced her journey, she noticed a shift in her relationships. Her newfound confidence and peace inspired those around her. Friends began to confide in her, drawn to her compassion and insight. Her mother, who had always been guarded about her emotions, opened up about her own struggles, deepening their bond. Olivia's journey through Psychic Hellfire became a beacon of hope, showing others that the flames could be transformative rather than destructive.

The Lesson of Psychic Hellfire

Olivia's story reveals that Psychic Hellfire is both a challenge and a gift. It is a transformative force that forces us to confront the interconnectedness of our mental, emotional, physical, and spiritual selves, pushing us to integrate and embrace our true nature. It's a journey of hope and inspiration, showing that even the most intense fires can lead to profound growth and healing.

Key Insights:

1. Integration is Key: Psychic Hellfire arises when unresolved aspects of the self collide. Healing requires addressing all dimensions of the fire. By embracing the process of integration, we can take control of our journey through Psychic Hellfire, empowering ourselves to heal and grow.
2. Sensitivity is Strength: What feels like a burden is often a profound gift waiting to be embraced.
3. Balance Brings Peace: Grounding practices like mindfulness, movement, and connection to purpose can transform the storm into a guiding light. By finding balance in all aspects of our being, we can navigate the storm of Psychic Hellfire with a sense of calm and reassurance, knowing that peace is within reach.

THE INTEGRATION: WALKING THROUGH THE FIRE

Definition Recap

The journey through Hellfire, in all its dimensions—mental, physical, emotional, spiritual, and psychic—is not one of destruction but of integration. The fires of life burn away illusions, cleanse the soul, and reveal the essence of who we are. When the flames of Hellfire intertwine, they forge a powerful force of transformation, offering the opportunity to emerge stronger, wiser, and more authentic.

Short Story: The Crucible of Wholeness

For years, Nathan had prided himself on his resilience. A successful entrepreneur, devoted father, and community leader, he was the kind of person others admired—steady, reliable, unshakable. But beneath the surface, cracks were forming.

It began subtly, with sleepless nights and a persistent ache in his chest. He chalked it up to stress, dismissing the whispers of unease. But then the panic attacks started. Out of nowhere, his heart would race, his breathing would quicken, and a wave of terror would wash over him. Nathan was no stranger to challenges, but this was different. This was a fire he couldn't control.

The Fires Collide

Nathan's descent into Hellfire was a perfect storm:

- Mental Hellfire ignited as his thoughts spiraled. He couldn't silence the voice that said he was failing—not just in his business but as a father, a husband, and a person.

- Physical Hellfire followed, manifesting in chronic migraines, muscle tension, and fatigue that no amount of rest could cure.
- Emotional Hellfire burned in his heart as he grappled with unspoken grief over the loss of his father years earlier, a wound he had buried beneath layers of work and distraction.
- Spiritual Hellfire smoldered in the background, leaving him questioning his purpose. The faith that had once been his anchor now felt like a distant memory.
- Psychic Hellfire erupted in unexpected ways. Nathan began having vivid dreams—images of fire, water, and a figure he couldn't quite make out calling his name. He dismissed them initially, but the dreams grew more intense, haunting him even in waking hours.

One night, the fires came to a head. Nathan found himself sitting alone in his office, staring at the photo of his father on his desk. The weight of everything—the expectations, the failures, the unspoken pain—came crashing down. He felt like he was burning from the inside out, the flames consuming every part of him.

"I can't do this anymore," he whispered.

The Turning Point

In that moment of surrender, something shifted. Nathan didn't realize it at the time, but admitting his vulnerability was the first step toward healing. The next day, he reached out to an old friend who had always seemed to have a way of grounding him. They met for coffee, and for the first time in years, Nathan allowed himself to open up.

His friend listened without judgment and then said something that stayed with Nathan: "You can't outrun the fire, but you can learn to walk through it. And when you do, you'll find it's not there to destroy you—it's there to transform you."

The Process of Integration

Nathan's journey through the fire was slow and unsteady but also profoundly transformative. He began to address each dimension of his Hellfire:

1. Mental: Through therapy, Nathan learned to challenge the negative thoughts that had taken root in his mind. He practiced mindfulness, finding moments of peace amidst the chaos.
2. Physical: He began prioritizing his health, incorporating yoga and regular exercise into his routine. He also learned to listen to his body, recognizing the connection between his physical and emotional symptoms.
3. Emotional: Nathan allowed himself to grieve, writing letters to his father that he would never send. He cried, screamed, and sat in silence, letting the emotions flow through him rather than suppressing them.
4. Spiritual: He reconnected with his faith, not through rigid practices but by finding moments of awe and wonder in everyday life—watching a sunrise, playing with his children, and simply breathing.
5. Psychic: Nathan began keeping a dream journal, exploring the messages his subconscious was sending. He realized that the figure in his dreams was a younger version of himself, reminding him of the curiosity and passion he had lost along the way.

The Fire Transformed

Months later, Nathan stood at the edge of a lake near his childhood home, where he and his father had spent countless summers fishing and talking about life. The sun was setting, painting the water in hues of gold and crimson. Nathan closed his eyes, breathing in the crisp air. The fire within him hadn't disappeared, but it had changed. It no longer consumed him—it fueled him.

For the first time in years, Nathan felt whole. The journey through Hellfire had burned away his fears, doubts, and the walls he had built around his heart. What remained was something purer, more substantial—a version of himself that he hadn't known existed.

The Ripple Effect

Nathan's transformation didn't just impact him—it rippled out to those around him. His relationships deepened as he showed up with more authenticity and vulnerability. His business thrived as he approached it with renewed clarity and purpose. And his children saw a father who wasn't afraid to feel, fail, and grow.

The Lesson of Integration

Nathan's story illustrates that Hellfire, in all its forms, is not a punishment but an opportunity. By confronting each dimension—mental, physical, emotional, spiritual, and psychic—we can integrate the lessons they offer and emerge stronger, wiser, and more aligned with our true selves.

Key Insights:

1. Surrender is Strength: Admitting vulnerability is not weakness—it is the first step toward transformation.
2. The Fire is a Teacher: Each dimension of Hellfire offers unique lessons that, when integrated, lead to profound growth.
3. Wholeness is Possible: Walking through the fire reveals that we are not broken but beautifully human, capable of healing and transformation.

Nathan's Journey Through the Fire

The Beginning of the Fall

Nathan's struggle didn't begin with the panic attacks—it had been building for years. As a child, he had always felt the weight of expectation. His father was a self-made man, the kind of person who believed in hard work and sacrifice above all else. Nathan adored his father, but he also feared disappointing him. Success became Nathan's measure of worth, and he carried that belief into adulthood.

For years, it worked. Nathan built a thriving business, married his college sweetheart, and became the kind of man others admired. But beneath the surface, he was stretched thin. The cracks in his carefully constructed life began to show after his father's death.

Nathan had always considered his father indestructible, a pillar of strength and wisdom. Losing him felt like losing the foundation of his life. But instead of grieving, Nathan threw himself into work, pushing harder than ever. "I'll honor his legacy by succeeding," he told himself, but the truth was, he was running from the pain.

The Ignition

The panic attacks started six months after his father's funeral. The first one hit him in a meeting. He was reviewing a quarterly report when, out of nowhere, his chest tightened. His heart raced, his hands went numb, and he felt like he couldn't breathe. Convinced he was having a heart attack, Nathan excused himself and rushed to the emergency room.

The doctors found nothing physically wrong. "It's probably stress," they said, but Nathan didn't believe them. He couldn't admit that the man who had always been in control was now unraveling. Over the next few months, the attacks became more frequent, leaving Nathan exhausted and frightened. He began avoiding situations that might trigger them, retreating further into himself.

The Fires Collide

Nathan's withdrawal took a toll on his family. His wife, Emily, tried to reach him, but every conversation ended in frustration. "I'm fine," he would insist, even as the fire inside him grew. His children noticed the change, too. "Why is Daddy always angry?" his youngest asked one evening, and the question cut Nathan to the core.

But it wasn't just the mental and emotional fires burning within him. The stress began to manifest physically. Migraines plagued him almost daily, and his back ached constantly. He was barely sleeping, and his dreams were vivid and unsettling when he did. He often saw his father, not as the strong man he remembered but as a frail figure standing in a burning field, reaching out to him.

Nathan began to question everything—his work, relationships, and faith. The God he had once turned to for guidance now felt silent and distant. What's the point of any of this? He wondered. Like a ship lost at sea, he felt adrift, surrounded by flames with no way out.

The Moment of Surrender

Nathan's breaking point came on a cold November evening. He was sitting alone in his office, staring at his father's watch—a gift he had inherited. It had stopped ticking when his father died, and Nathan had never bothered to fix it. To him, it felt symbolic, a reminder that time had somehow frozen on that day.

For hours, he sat there, the weight of his grief, guilt, and fear pressing down on him. Finally, the dam broke. He wept—loud, gut-wrenching sobs that echoed through the empty house. "I can't do this anymore," he whispered, the words trembling on his lips.

At that moment, something shifted. For the first time, Nathan stopped fighting the fire. He allowed himself to feel the full weight of his pain, his loss, and his fear. He didn't try to analyze it or push it away. He let it be.

The Path Forward

The following day, Nathan called his friend Greg, whom he hadn't spoken to in months. Greg was the kind of person who had a way of grounding people, and Nathan needed that now more than ever. Over coffee, he poured out everything—the panic attacks, the grief, the dreams, and the growing sense of disconnection.

Greg listened without judgment and said, "Nathan, you're carrying too much. You've been trying to outrun the fire, but you can't. The only way out is through."

Those words stuck with Nathan. That evening, he wrote them down in a notebook and resolved to begin his journey through the fire. He started small—therapy sessions once a week, daily walks without phone use, and ten minutes of quiet reflection each morning. The changes initially felt insignificant, but they added up over time.

The Fires Tamed

In therapy, Nathan explored the root of his Mental Hellfire—the belief that his worth was tied to his achievements. He realized how much of his identity had been shaped by his father's expectations and how he had internalized them as his own. He began redefining success as not a constant achievement but as living authentically and purposefully.

Through journaling, Nathan confronted his Emotional Hellfire. He wrote letters to his father, expressing the anger and sadness he had buried for years. He allowed himself to grieve, not just for his father but for the version of himself he had lost along the way.

Yoga and meditation helped him address his Physical Hellfire, teaching him to release tension and reconnect with his body. And as he reconnected with his spirituality, he found peace in the idea that not all questions needed answers. The silence he had feared became a space for reflection and growth.

The Integration

Months later, Nathan returned to the lake, where he and his father spent many summers. He brought the watch that had stopped ticking and a notebook filled with letters to his father. As the sun set, painting the water in shades of gold and crimson, Nathan read the letters aloud, letting the words carry into the wind.

When he finished, he placed the letters and the watch into a small fire he had built by the shore. He watched as the flames consumed them, feeling a sense of release and renewal. The fire that had once threatened to destroy him had become a source of transformation, leaving him firmer, wiser, and more whole.

The Ripple Effect

Nathan's journey changed not just him but everyone around him. His openness inspired Emily to confront her unspoken struggles, deepening their bond. His children saw a new side of their father—vulnerable yet strong, a man unafraid to feel and grow. Even his business benefited as Nathan approached it with renewed clarity and purpose.

The Lesson of Nathan's Journey

Nathan's story is a testament to the power of integration. By confronting each aspect of Hellfire—mental, physical, emotional, spiritual, and psychic—he emerged transformed. His journey reminds us that the fire is not our enemy but our teacher, guiding us toward wholeness.

Key Insights:

Surrender is Strength: Letting go of the need to control is the first step toward healing.

Healing is Holistic: True transformation requires addressing all dimensions of the self.

The Fire Refines: The flames of Hellfire burn away what no longer serves us, revealing our true essence.

Nathan's Transformation: From Ashes to Strength

The First Steps into the Fire

After his conversation with Greg, Nathan's first step was acknowledging that his panic attacks weren't random. They were the body's urgent message that his life, as it was, couldn't continue. That realization alone felt like a revelation. Nathan had been ignoring the whispers of discomfort for years, but now those whispers had become a deafening roar. The first therapy session was more complicated than he expected.

Nathan sat across from his therapist, a calm and steady woman named Diane, who began with a simple question: "What brings you here today?"

For a moment, Nathan couldn't speak. The answer seemed too vast, too complicated to put into words. Finally, he said, "I feel like I'm falling apart. And I don't know how to stop it."

Diane nodded, her expression kind. "Occasionally falling apart is the first step toward coming together."

Facing the Mental Hellfire

In the following weeks, Nathan began unpacking his Mental Hellfire's layers. He explored the deeply ingrained belief that his worth was tied to his productivity and success. Diane helped him trace it back to his childhood, where his father's words—meant to inspire—had instead instilled a relentless drive for perfection.

Nathan remembered moments he had long buried: when he came home with a 95 on a math test, only for his father to ask, "What happened to the other five points?" Or the day he won a track meet, his father said, "You'll have to work twice as hard next time to keep that title."

Diane didn't let him stop there. "What do you think your father was trying to teach you?" she asked.

Nathan thought about it for a long time. "I think he wanted me to be strong. To never settle. But it made me feel like I was never enough."

Diane nodded. "That strength he valued—it's in you. But it doesn't have to come at the cost of your peace. Let's work on redefining what strength looks like for you."

Through their sessions, Nathan began challenging the critical voice in his head. He practiced mindfulness, learning to recognize the thoughts that spiraled into self-doubt and replacing them with affirmations of self-worth. It wasn't easy—sometimes, the old thoughts returned with a vengeance—but slowly, the fire in his mind began to quiet.

THE WEAVING OF THE FIRES

NATHAN'S JOURNEY AS A UNIVERSAL MIRROR

Confronting the Emotional Hellfire

The most painful part of Nathan's journey came when he turned to his Emotional Hellfire. For years, he had buried his grief over his father's death, focusing instead on his business and his family. But the grief hadn't disappeared—it had festered, becoming a smoldering ember that fueled his other struggles.

In one session, Diane asked Nathan to describe his father in three words. Without hesitation, Nathan said, "Strong, determined, proud."

"And if he were sitting here with us today," Diane continued, "what do you think he'd say about you?"

Nathan's throat tightened. He looked away, blinking back tears. "I don't know. I want to think he'd be proud of me. But… I don't know if I've done enough."

"Enough for what?" Diane asked gently.

Nathan couldn't answer. The question lingered in his mind long after the session ended.

That night, Nathan wrote a letter to his father. At first, the words came haltingly, but soon they poured out—his anger, sadness, and longing for the man who had shaped him in many ways. "I wish you'd told me it was okay to fail," he wrote. "I wish you'd told me it was okay to rest. But I know now that I must believe those things for myself."

As he finished the letter, a sense of release washed over him. For the first time, he felt the weight of his grief begin to lift.

RELEASING THE PHYSICAL HELLFIRE

Nathan's physical transformation began with minor changes. Diane encouraged him to reconnect with his body, not as a machine to be optimized but as a partner in his healing. He started yoga, though he felt awkward at first. His body, stiff from years of neglect, resisted the movements. But as the weeks passed, he felt a sense of ease he hadn't known in years.

He also started walking each morning, leaving his phone behind to be present simply. The walks became a form of meditation, a way to process his thoughts and emotions without distraction. On those walks, he often felt his father's presence—not as a judgmental voice but as a quiet encouragement, a reminder of their shared connection.

Rekindling the Spiritual Flame

Nathan's spiritual journey was perhaps the most surprising. He had grown up with a strong sense of faith, but his father's death had left him questioning everything. For months, he had felt abandoned by the divine, as though the universe had turned its back on him.

But one evening, during a walk by the lake, something shifted. The sun was setting, casting the water in shades of gold and orange. Nathan stopped and closed his eyes, breathing in the cool air. At that moment, he felt an overwhelming sense of peace. It wasn't a dramatic revelation—it was quiet, gentle, like a whisper in his heart. You are not alone.

From then on, Nathan approached his spirituality with curiosity rather than obligation. He began meditating, not to find answers but to embrace the mystery. He found moments of awe in the small things—a bird's song, a child's laughter, the way sunlight filtered through the trees. These moments became his prayers, his way of reconnecting with the divine.

The Final Integration

Months later, Nathan stood in his father's workshop, which he hadn't visited since the funeral. Dust coated the tools, and the air smelled faintly of sawdust and oil. He found a half-finished project on the workbench—an old clock his father had been restoring.

Nathan picked it up, running his fingers over the worn wood. He smiled, remembering how his father had always said, "Every broken thing can be fixed if you're willing to put in the time."

Nathan finished the clock that day, taking time to sand, polish, and assemble the pieces. When he hung it on the wall, its steady ticking filled the room. It wasn't just a clock—a symbol of his journey, a reminder that there is beauty and possibility even in brokenness.

NATHAN: THE RIPPLE EFFECT

Nathan's transformation radiated outward, touching everyone around him. His wife, Emily, noticed the change immediately. "You're different," she said one evening as they sat together on the porch. "It's like… you're more here."

"I think I am," Nathan replied, taking her hand. "And I'm not going anywhere."

His children saw a new side of their father—a man who laughed more, admitted when he was wrong, and wasn't afraid to say, "I don't know, but we'll figure it out together."

At work, Nathan's renewed clarity inspired his team, fostering a culture of collaboration and support. But perhaps most importantly, Nathan found peace within himself—a peace that no success or achievement could ever replicate.

The Fires Intertwined

Nathan's story is a tale of personal transformation and a reflection of the universal human experience. His journey through Hellfire in its mental, physical, emotional, spiritual, and psychic dimensions reveals the interconnectedness of these aspects of existence. Each flame illuminates a different part of his soul, creating a crucible for profound change.

But Nathan's path is not unique. It is the story of every individual who faces the fire and chooses to walk through it. By weaving his journey with the larger tapestry of life's struggles and triumphs, we can uncover deeper truths about the cycles of failure, renewal, and spiritual understanding that define our existence.

The Cycle of Hellfire

The Breaking Point: Recognizing the Cycle

Nathan's collapse began with a single point of ignition—his father's death. But the fire that consumed him was not born at that moment. It had been smoldering for years, hidden beneath layers of achievement, responsibility, and unexamined beliefs. This is the nature of the cycle of Hellfire: it builds silently, unnoticed until a single spark sets it ablaze.

For Nathan, the spark was grief—a grief he didn't know how to process. His father's death brought to the surface every suppressed emotion, every unspoken fear, every unresolved question about his life and purpose. The fire revealed the cracks in his carefully constructed identity, forcing him to confront the truth he had been avoiding: that his sense of self was fragile, built on external validation rather than inner understanding.

THE DESCENT: FACING THE FLAMES

The descent into Hellfire is marked by resistance. Nathan resisted his pain, his vulnerability, and his growing sense of disconnection. He tried to maintain control, to push through the flames as he had always done. But the fire does not allow for shortcuts. It demands surrender.

In this phase, Nathan experienced the full force of the intertwined fires:

- Mental Hellfire consumed him with thoughts of failure and inadequacy.
- Physical Hellfire manifested as chronic pain and exhaustion, his body mirroring the turmoil of his mind.
- Emotional Hellfire burned in the form of unexpressed grief and anger, emotions he had buried for years.
- Spiritual Hellfire left him questioning his faith and purpose, feeling abandoned by the divine.
- Psychic Hellfire emerged through vivid dreams and an overwhelming sense of energetic disarray.

Each dimension fed into the others, creating a cycle of suffering that felt inescapable. This is the nature of Hellfire: it isolates, overwhelms, and consumes—until we stop running from it.

The Turning Point: Surrender and Acceptance

Nathan's breakthrough came not from a moment of triumph but from a moment of surrender. On the night he wept in his office, he allowed himself to feel the full weight of his pain for the first time. This act of vulnerability was the key to breaking the cycle.

In this context, surrender is not defeat. It is the recognition that the fire is not an enemy but a teacher. Nathan's tears were an acknowledgment of his humanity, imperfection, and need for connection. By allowing himself to feel, he began to release the emotions and beliefs fueling the fire.

The Integration: Walking Through the Fire

Nathan's journey through the fire was a process of integration—a weaving together of the fragmented parts of himself. Each dimension of Hellfire required its form of healing, but the lessons were interconnected:

1. **Mental Hellfire** taught Nathan to challenge his inner critic and redefine success. He realized that his worth was not tied to his achievements but to his authenticity and integrity.
2. **Physical Hellfire** forced him to reconnect with his body, teaching him to listen to its signals and honor its needs.
3. **Emotional Hellfire** revealed the power of vulnerability. By expressing his grief and anger, Nathan began to heal the wounds he had carried for years.
4. **Spiritual Hellfire** reignited his faith—not as a set of rigid beliefs but as a relationship with the mystery and wonder of existence.
5. **Psychic Hellfire** awakened his intuition, helping him trust his inner voice's guidance and the interconnectedness of all things.

Through this integration, Nathan emerged transformed. His fears or his failures no longer define him. Instead, he embraced his imperfections as a source of strength and his struggles as a pathway to wisdom.

THE SPIRITUAL UNDERSTANDING

THE INFINITE CYCLE

The Nature of Failure

Nathan's journey revealed a profound truth about failure: it is not an endpoint but a beginning. In the life cycle, failure is the spark that ignites the fire of transformation. It burns away the illusions of control and perfection, revealing the essence of who we are.

For Nathan, failure was a gift. It forced him to confront the beliefs and patterns that no longer served him, let go of what was holding him back, and rebuild his life on a foundation of truth and resilience. In this way, failure became a doorway to spiritual growth—a reminder that we are not defined by our mistakes but by how we respond to them.

The Fires Intertwined

Nathan's story is not a tale of personal transformation but a reflection of the universal human experience. His journey through Hellfire in its mental, physical, emotional, spiritual, and psychic dimensions reveals the interconnectedness of these aspects of existence. Each flame illuminates a different part of his soul, creating a crucible for profound change.

But Nathan's path is not unique. It is the story of every individual who faces the fire and chooses to walk through it. By weaving his journey with the larger tapestry of life's struggles and triumphs, we can uncover deeper truths about the cycles of failure, renewal, and spiritual understanding that define our existence.

The Cycle of Hellfire

The Breaking Point: Recognizing the Cycle

Nathan's collapse began with a single point of ignition—his father's death. But the fire that consumed him was not born at that moment. It had been smoldering for years, hidden beneath layers of achievement, responsibility, and unexamined beliefs. This is the nature of the cycle of Hellfire: it builds silently, unnoticed until a single spark sets it ablaze.

For Nathan, the spark was grief—a grief he didn't know how to process. His father's death brought to the surface every suppressed emotion, every unspoken fear, every unresolved question about his life and purpose. The fire revealed the cracks in his carefully constructed identity, forcing him to confront the truth he had been avoiding: that his sense of self was fragile, built on external validation rather than inner understanding.

The Descent: Facing the Flames

The descent into Hellfire is marked by resistance. Nathan resisted his pain, his vulnerability, and his growing sense of disconnection. He tried to maintain control, to push through the flames as he had always done. But the fire does not allow for shortcuts. It demands surrender.

In this phase, Nathan experienced the full force of the intertwined fires:

- **Mental Hellfire** consumed him with thoughts of failure and inadequacy.
- **Physical Hellfire** manifested as chronic pain and exhaustion, his body mirroring the turmoil of his mind.
- **Emotional Hellfire** burned in the form of unexpressed grief and anger, emotions he had buried for years.
- **Spiritual Hellfire** left him questioning his faith and purpose, feeling abandoned by the divine.
- **Psychic Hellfire** emerged through vivid dreams and an overwhelming sense of energetic disarray.

Each dimension fed into the others, creating a cycle of suffering that felt inescapable. This is the nature of Hellfire: it isolates, overwhelms, and consumes—until we stop running from it.

The Turning Point: Surrender and Acceptance

Nathan's breakthrough came not from a moment of triumph but from a moment of surrender. On the night he wept in his office, he allowed himself to feel the full weight of his pain for the first time. This act of vulnerability was the key to breaking the cycle.

In this context, surrender is not defeat. It is the recognition that the fire is not an enemy but a teacher. Nathan's tears were an acknowledgment of his humanity, imperfection, and need for connection. By allowing himself to feel, he began to release the emotions and beliefs fueling the fire.

The Integration: Walking Through the Fire

Nathan's journey through the fire was a process of integration—a weaving together of the fragmented parts of himself. Each dimension of Hellfire required its form of healing, but the lessons were interconnected:

1. **Mental Hellfire** taught Nathan to challenge his inner critic and redefine success. He realized that his worth was not tied to his achievements but to his authenticity and integrity.
2. **Physical** Hellfire forced him to reconnect with his body, teaching him to listen to its signals and honor its needs.
3. **Emotional Hellfire** revealed the power of vulnerability. By expressing his grief and anger, Nathan began to heal the wounds he had carried for years.
4. **Spiritual Hellfire** reignited his faith—not as a set of rigid beliefs but as a relationship with the mystery and wonder of existence.
5. **Psychic Hellfire** awakened his intuition, helping him trust his inner voice's guidance and the interconnectedness of all things.

Through this integration, Nathan emerged transformed. His fears or his failures no longer define him. Instead, he embraced his imperfections as a source of strength and his struggles as a pathway to wisdom.

The Spiritual Understanding: The Infinite Cycle

The Nature of Failure

Nathan's journey revealed a profound truth about failure: it is not an endpoint but a beginning. In the life cycle, failure is the spark that ignites the fire of transformation. It burns away the illusions of control and perfection, revealing the essence of who we are.

For Nathan, failure was a gift. It forced him to confront the beliefs and patterns that no longer served him, let go of what was holding him back, and rebuild his life on a foundation of truth and resilience. In this way, failure became a doorway to spiritual growth—a reminder that we are not defined by our mistakes but by how we respond to them.

The Soul's Journey

Nathan's experience also illuminated the deeper cycles of the soul's journey. Each stage of his transformation mirrored a universal process:

1. **Ignition:** The spark of Hellfire, often triggered by loss or change, disrupts the status quo.
2. **Descent:** The confrontation with pain, fear, and uncertainty—a necessary step in growth.
3. **Surrender:** The moment of acceptance, when resistance gives way to vulnerability and openness.
4. **Integration:** Weaving lessons creates a more profound sense of wholeness.
5. **Renewal:** The emergence from the fire, transformed and ready to embrace life with greater clarity and purpose.

This cycle is infinite, repeating throughout our lives as we grow and evolve. Each journey through the fire brings us closer to understanding our true nature and connection to the divine.

The Ripple Effect: The Universal Mirror

Nathan's transformation was profoundly personal but reflected a universal truth: We all walk through the fire in our ways. His story serves as a mirror, showing us that our struggles are not isolated or meaningless. They are part of a larger tapestry—a collective journey of growth and awakening.

By sharing his journey, Nathan became a source of light for others. His vulnerability inspired his family, his openness deepened his relationships, and his wisdom enriched his community. In this way, his transformation became a ripple that extended far beyond himself, touching the lives of everyone around him.

Conclusion: The Fire as a Gift

Nathan's journey through Hellfire teaches us that fire is not something to fear but to embrace. It is a gift—a force that strips away the superficial and reveals our true identity. Walking through the fire, we discover our strength, wisdom, and capacity for renewal.

Key Takeaways:

1. Failure is a Catalyst: It sparks the fire of transformation, breaking down the old to make way for the new.
2. Integration is Essential: True healing requires addressing all dimensions of the self—mental, physical, emotional, spiritual, and psychic.
3. The Fire is Universal: Nathan's story is our story. We are all walking through the fire, and in doing so, we are all becoming more whole.

Expanded Framework: The Journey Through Hellfire

Introduction to the Framework

The journey through Hellfire is not a singular path but a multi-dimensional experience that integrates the mental, physical, emotional, spiritual, and psychic aspects of being. Each dimension of Hellfire reflects a unique challenge, yet all are interconnected, forming a crucible for profound transformation. To expand Nathan's story into a universal framework, we must delve deeper into the cycles of ignition, descent, surrender, integration, and renewal, revealing how they guide us toward growth and spiritual understanding.

THE FIVE PILLARS OF HELLFIRE

1. Mental Hellfire: The Maze of the Mind

- **Core Challenge:** Confronting self-doubt, fear, and limiting beliefs.
- **Cycle:**
  - **Ignition:** A life event triggers relentless overthinking and mental anguish.
  - **Descent:** The mind spirals into negativity, amplifying internal conflicts.
  - **Surrender:** Acceptance of the mind's chatter without judgment, opening the door to change.
  - **Integration:** Reframing limiting beliefs and replacing them with empowering truths.
  - **Renewal:** Emergence of clarity, focus, and mental freedom.
  - **Framework Integration:** Nathan's mental spiral, driven by his belief that worth was tied to success, illustrates how Mental Hellfire often masks deeper insecurities. His journey to challenge these beliefs and embrace imperfection offers a roadmap for others navigating this dimension.

2. Physical Hellfire: The Body's Call to Attention

- **Core Challenge:** Recognizing the body as a vessel for unresolved pain and stress.
- **Cycle:**
  - **Ignition:** Physical symptoms—chronic pain, fatigue, or illness—manifest as a signal.
  - **Descent:** Neglect and avoidance exacerbate the body's distress.
  - **Surrender:** Listening to the body, acknowledging its needs, and treating it carefully.
  - **Integration:** Adopting practices like movement, nutrition, and rest that restore balance.

- **Renewal:** Reconnection with the body as an ally in healing and growth.
- **Framework Integration:** Nathan's back pain and migraines were physical manifestations of his emotional and mental burdens. His yoga practice and mindful walks demonstrated the importance of treating the body as an integral part of the healing journey.

3. Emotional Hellfire: The Heart's Inferno

- **Core Challenge:** Allowing suppressed emotions to surface and be expressed.
- **Cycle:**

- **Ignition:** A loss or betrayal brings unresolved emotions to the forefront.
- **Descent:** The weight of grief, anger, or shame threatens to consume.
- **Surrender:** Vulnerability becomes a tool for releasing emotional pain.
- **Integration:** Emotions are processed and transformed into wisdom.
- **Renewal:** A lighter heart and the ability to connect deeply with others.
- **Framework Integration:** Nathan's grief for his father revealed how buried emotions fuel the other dimensions of Hellfire. His letter-writing practice and tearful surrender illustrate the healing power of emotional expression.

4. Spiritual Hellfire: The Dark Night of the Soul

- **Core Challenge:** Navigating the loss of faith, purpose, or connection to the divine.
- **Cycle:**

- **Ignition:** A life crisis shakes one's foundational beliefs.
- **Descent:** A sense of abandonment by the divine or existential disconnection.

- o **Surrender:** Embracing uncertainty and seeking meaning beyond dogma.
- o **Integration:** Rebuilding faith through wonder, gratitude, and interconnectedness.
- o **Renewal:** A deeper, more authentic relationship with the spiritual self.
- o **Framework Integration:** Nathan's spiritual crisis, symbolized by his dreams and feelings of divine silence, showcases how Spiritual Hellfire strips away shallow beliefs to reveal profound truths. His rediscovery of awe and gratitude became a cornerstone of his renewal.

5. Psychic Hellfire: The Energetic Awakening

- **Core Challenge:** Managing heightened sensitivity to unseen forces and energies.
- **Cycle:**

- o **Ignition:** Sudden intuitive or paranormal experiences disrupt one's sense of reality.
- o **Descent:** Overwhelming and confusion about energetic or psychic phenomena.
- o **Surrender:** Accepting sensitivity as a gift rather than a burden.
- o **Integration:** Developing practices to ground and harness intuitive abilities.
- o **Renewal:** A heightened awareness of the interconnectedness of all things.
- o **Framework Integration:** Although initially unsettling, Nathan's vivid dreams and intuitive insights became a guiding force in his journey. His dream journal and meditation practice helped him harness these energies as tools for growth.

The Interconnected Fires

The five dimensions of Hellfire are not isolated—they are deeply intertwined. For Nathan, his mental self-criticism fueled his emotional pain, which manifested as physical tension. His spiritual doubts exacerbated his psychic sensitivity, creating a storm that touched every aspect of his being. This interplay reveals the holistic nature of Hellfire: true transformation requires addressing all dimensions simultaneously.

The Universal Cycle of Renewal

Nathan's journey illustrates the cyclical nature of Hellfire. Each stage—ignition, descent, surrender, integration, and renewal—builds upon the last, creating a continuous growth process. This cycle is not linear but recursive; we revisit the fire at different stages of life, each time emerging with new insights and strength.

Deeper Spiritual Understanding: The Purpose of Hellfire

The Soul's Refinement

Hellfire is the soul's crucible, a necessary process of purification and transformation. It stomps away the false identities we cling to and reveals the essence of who we are. For Nathan, the fire burned away his need for external validation, leaving behind a man who valued authenticity, connection, and purpose.

The Divine Connection

Hellfire also serves as a bridge to the divine. In the depths of his despair, Nathan rediscovered his faith—not as a rigid set of beliefs but as a relationship with the infinite. This shift allowed him to see the divine in everyday moments, transforming his life into a prayer of gratitude and wonder.

The Collective Journey

Finally, Hellfire is a collective experience. Nathan's transformation rippled outward, touching the lives of his family, friends, and community. This reflects a universal truth: our individual growth contributes to the greater whole, inspiring and uplifting those around us.

The Framework's Application

1. **For Individuals:** This framework guides navigating life's challenges, offering tools and insights for transformation.
2. **For Communities:** By sharing stories like Nathan's, we create a sense of connection and purpose, reminding others that they are not alone in their journey.
3. **For Spiritual Growth:** The framework encourages a holistic approach to healing, integrating all dimensions of the self to achieve wholeness.

Weaving Additional Stories Into the Framework

To create a richer, more universal narrative, let's weave additional stories that illustrate the different dimensions of Hellfire and their interplay. Each story will highlight unique challenges while reinforcing the framework's interconnectedness. These narratives will serve as mirrors for readers, helping them see their struggles and triumphs in a broader, more relatable context.

1. Mental Hellfire: Sarah's Battle with Perfection

Ignition

Sarah was the epitome of success—an executive at a top firm, a mother of two, and a marathon runner. On the surface, she had it all together. But beneath the polished exterior, Sarah drowned in her need for Perfection. Every email she sent, every presentation she delivered, every parenting decision she made—each was scrutinized relentlessly by her inner critic.

Her breaking point came during a quarterly review. Her boss praised her stellar performance but mentioned one minor typo in a report. That single comment ignited a firestorm in Sarah's mind. How could I have missed that? They'll think I'm incompetent.

Descent

Sarah's thoughts spiraled into a relentless cycle of doubt and self-criticism. She stopped sleeping, lying awake at night, replaying every perceived mistake. Her mental turmoil began to affect her relationships; she snapped at her children over small messes and avoided her friends, too ashamed to admit how overwhelmed she felt.

Surrender and Integration

One day, Sarah attended a mindfulness workshop at her company, skeptical but desperate for relief. During a guided meditation, the instructor said, "Perfection is a myth. Strive for authenticity instead." The words struck a chord. Sarah realized her inner critic echoed her childhood, where praise was conditional and mistakes were unforgivable.

Through therapy and mindfulness, Sarah began challenging her perfectionist tendencies. She learned to celebrate her achievements, forgive her mistakes, and approach life with curiosity instead of fear. Slowly, the flames of Mental Hellfire began to dim.

2. Physical Hellfire: Carlos's Silent Pain

Ignition

Carlos had been a carpenter for over 30 years, and his body bore the marks of his labor—calloused hands, aching joints, and a persistent pain in his lower back. He ignored the pain for years, dismissing it as a natural part of aging. But one morning, as he bent down to pick up a toolbox, a sharp, searing pain shot through his spine. He collapsed, unable to move.

Descent

Carlos's world shrank. He could no longer work, which left him feeling useless. The pain consumed him, radiating through his body and clouding his mind. Friends and family tried to help, but Carlos pushed them away, ashamed of his vulnerability.

Surrender and Integration

Carlos's turning point came during a visit to a physical therapist who asked him, "Do you see your body as a partner or an obstacle?" The question forced Carlos to confront how he had neglected his body for decades, treating it as a tool rather than a part of himself.

Through gentle exercises and bodywork, Carlos began reconnecting with his physical self. He also joined a support group for chronic pain sufferers, where he learned to share his struggles without shame. Over time, Carlos regained mobility and a newfound respect for his body and its resilience.

3. Emotional Hellfire: Priya's Journey Through Grief

Ignition

Priya's world shattered the day her husband, Raj, passed away unexpectedly. The grief was immediate and overwhelming, a tidal wave of pain that left her gasping for air. Friends and family surrounded her with love, but their words of comfort—"He's in a better place," or "Time heals all wounds"—felt hollow.

Descent

Months passed, but Priya's grief didn't subside. She isolated herself, afraid that her sorrow would burden others. Every corner of her home reminded her of Raj—the scent of his cologne, the half-finished novel on his nightstand. She felt trapped in a house of memories, unable to move forward yet unable to let go.

Surrender and Integration

One evening, Priya stumbled upon Raj's old journal. In it, she found a quote he had underlined: "Grief is the price we pay for love." The words brought tears to her eyes and a sense of acceptance. She realized that her grief wasn't something to escape—it was a testament to the depth of her love.

Priya began attending a grief support group, where she found solace in sharing her story and hearing others. Slowly, she transformed her pain into a source of strength, finding ways to honor Raj's memory while embracing life again.

4. Spiritual Hellfire: Ahmed's Crisis of Faith

Ignition

For years, Ahmed had been a devoted man of faith, following the teachings of his religion with unwavering discipline. However, after his daughter was diagnosed with a chronic illness, Ahmed's faith began to waver. He prayed for her healing, but the answers didn't come. Instead, he felt abandoned by the God he had always trusted.

Descent

Ahmed's crisis of faith left him adrift. He stopped attending prayers, unable to reconcile his beliefs with his daughter's suffering. The spiritual community he had once relied on now felt alien, their reassurances hollow. He felt like he was wandering in a spiritual desert, parched and lost.

Surrender and Integration

Ahmed's turning point came during a late-night conversation with his daughter. She said, "Papa, even if I'm sick, I'm happy. Isn't that a blessing too?" Her words pierced Ahmed's despair, reminding him that faith wasn't about having all the answers but about finding gratitude amid uncertainty.

He began exploring his spirituality in a new way, focusing on gratitude, service, and the beauty of everyday moments. His faith, once rigid, became a fluid and personal connection with the divine.

5. Psychic Hellfire: Elise's Awakening

Ignition

Elise had always been skeptical, dismissing anything that logic couldn't explain. But after a near-death experience in a car accident, she began having vivid dreams and premonitions. She started sensing people's emotions, often before they spoke. The intensity of these experiences left her overwhelmed and frightened.

Descent

Elise tried to ignore her newfound sensitivity, but the visions became more persistent. She felt like she was losing her grip on reality. Friends dismissed her experiences as imagination, which left Elise feeling isolated and misunderstood.

Surrender and Integration

Elise found a mentor in a local healer who helped her understand her gifts. "Your sensitivity is not a curse," the healer said. "It's a call to expand your understanding of the world." With guidance, Elise learned grounding techniques and began using her intuition to help others, finding purpose in her abilities.

Bringing the Stories Together

These additional stories, woven with Nathan's, create a tapestry of transformation. Each narrative highlights a unique dimension of Hellfire while reinforcing the interconnectedness of the human experience. Together, they show that Hellfire, though painful, is a universal force for growth and renewal.

HELLFIRE AS A CONSTANT COMPANION

Hellfire is not limited to life's monumental challenges; its flames flicker in the small, everyday moments that test our patience, resilience, and sense of self. The interconnected fires—mental, physical, emotional, spiritual, and psychic—continually shape our experiences and influence our choices. Understanding how these dimensions weave into daily life allows us to navigate them with greater awareness and intentionality.

The Impact of Hellfire on Daily Life

1. Mental Hellfire: The Noise of Modern Living

In today's fast-paced world, Mental Hellfire thrives in the form of overthinking, anxiety, and information overload. Consider Sarah's experience from our earlier story, in which her inner critic scrutinized her actions. Her struggle mirrors the daily battles many face:

- **Work Stress:** Deadlines, performance reviews, and the pressure to excel ignite mental anguish.
- **Social Media:** Comparing oneself to curated images of perfection fuels self-doubt.
- **Decision Fatigue:** The constant need to make significant and small choices can paralyze the mind.

Integration in Daily Life: Practicing mindfulness and setting boundaries with technology can quiet the mental fire. Simple habits like journaling, taking breaks, and engaging in creative activities help reframe the narrative of self-criticism.

2. Physical Hellfire: The Body's Unheard Pleas

The demands of daily life often lead to neglect of the body. Carlos's back pain is a universal story—how usually do we ignore our physical needs in the name of productivity?

- **Sedentary Lifestyles:** Long hours at a desk lead to tension and discomfort.
- **Poor Nutrition:** Fast food and skipped meals rob the body of vitality.
- **Chronic Stress:** Physical symptoms like headaches and fatigue often go unaddressed.

Integration in Daily Life: Regular movement, nourishing food, and moments of rest restore balance. Listening to the body's signals—whether through stretching during work breaks or prioritizing sleep—prevents minor aches from becoming raging fires.

3. Emotional Hellfire: The Weight of Suppressed Feelings

Emotional Hellfire often smolders beneath the surface, fueled by unexpressed anger, sadness, or fear. Priya's grief over her husband highlights how emotional suppression affects daily life:

- **Relationship Strain:** Unspoken emotions lead to misunderstandings and disconnection.
- **Irritability:** Small frustrations explode into more significant conflicts when emotions are bottled up.
- **Loss of Joy:** Carrying unprocessed feelings dulls life's vibrancy.

Integration in Daily Life: Creating space for emotional expression—journaling, talking with a trusted friend, or engaging in therapy—helps release the fire. Daily gratitude practices and acts of kindness can also shift the emotional energy from pain to healing.

4. Spiritual Hellfire: The Quest for Meaning

In the busyness of modern life, Spiritual Hellfire often manifests as a quiet yearning—a sense that something is missing. Ahmed's crisis of faith mirrors the struggles many face:

- **Existential Questions:** Daily routines feel empty without a sense of purpose.
- **Disconnecting from Nature:** Urban environments and technology create barriers between people and the natural world, where many find spiritual renewal.
- **Lack of Ritual:** Spiritual practices can feel distant or irrelevant without grounding rituals.

Integration in Daily Life: Small, meaningful rituals—lighting a candle, walking in nature, or pausing to appreciate a sunset—reignite the spiritual flame. Practicing gratitude and seeking moments of awe in the ordinary deepen the connection to the divine.

5. Psychic Hellfire: The Overwhelming Energies

Daily life can feel like a constant storm for those sensitive to energy. Elise's story illustrates the challenges of navigating heightened intuition:

- **Energetic Overload:** Crowded spaces or emotionally charged environments can drain energy.
- **Difficulty Setting** Boundaries: Absorbing others' emotions leads to burnout.
- **Uncertainty:** Intuitive insights, while powerful, can feel confusing without guidance.

Integration in Daily Life: Grounding techniques like meditation, breathwork, and time in nature help balance psychic sensitivity. Setting energetic boundaries—such as visualizing protective light or limiting exposure to negative influences—empowers intuitive individuals.

Interweaving the Fires in Daily Life

Daily life rarely isolates one dimension of Hellfire. Instead, the fires intertwine, creating complex challenges that require holistic solutions. Consider these scenarios:

Example 1: The Overwhelmed Parent

Lisa is a working mother juggling deadlines, school pickups, and household chores. Her Mental Hellfire burns with thoughts of inadequacy, while her Physical Hellfire manifests as exhaustion. Emotional Hellfire adds guilt for not spending enough quality time with her children.

Integration:

- **Mental:** Lisa practices self-compassion, reminding herself she's doing her best.
- **Physical:** She commits to a nightly stretching routine to release tension.
- **Emotional:** Lisa introduces a "gratitude jar" with her children, focusing on positive moments rather than guilt.

Example 2: The Burned-Out Professional

Jason, a mid-level manager, questions the purpose of his work. Spiritual Hellfire leaves him feeling disconnected, while Mental Hellfire amplifies his doubts about his career. His Emotional Hellfire simmers with frustration he hasn't expressed to his boss.

Integration:

- **Spiritual:** Jason begins a morning meditation practice, focusing on gratitude and intention.
- **Mental:** He sets small, achievable goals to regain a sense of accomplishment.
- **Emotional:** Jason schedules a meeting with his boss to discuss his concerns, fostering clarity and relief.

Lessons from Hellfire in Daily Life

1. **Hellfire is a Messenger:** Each dimension of Hellfire signals an area of life that needs attention and care. By listening to these signals, we can address issues before they become overwhelming.
2. **Small Changes Have Big Impacts**: Simple, consistent practices—whether journaling, walking, or meditating—can transform daily struggles into opportunities for growth.
3. **Integration is Key:** Addressing all dimensions of the fire—mental, physical, emotional, spiritual, and psychic—leads to holistic healing and balance.

Conclusion: Living with the Fire

Hellfire is not something to be extinguished but to be embraced. Its flames, though intense, illuminate the path to self-awareness, growth, and connection. By weaving its lessons into daily life, we can transform the fire from a force of destruction into a source of light.

Weaving the Lessons of Hellfire into Daily Life:

Transforming Fire into Light

Introduction: The Fire as a Companion

The flames of Hellfire—mental, physical, emotional, spiritual, and psychic—are challenges to overcome and opportunities to grow. When we resist the fire, it consumes us, leaving destruction in its wake. But when we embrace it, the fire becomes a guiding light, illuminating truths about ourselves, our relationships, and the world around us. By weaving its lessons into daily life, we transform Hellfire from a force of chaos into a source of wisdom and strength.

The Practices of Transformation

To integrate the lessons of Hellfire into daily life, we must adopt practices that honor its dimensions. Each practice becomes a thread in the tapestry of transformation, creating a resilient and radiant life.

1. Mental Clarity: Calming the Inner Storm

Hellfire's mental dimension often manifests as overthinking, self-doubt, or negative thought spirals. We must quiet the mind and reshape our mental narrative to transform this fire.

Daily Practices:

- **Morning Affirmations:** Begin the day with empowering statements like, "I am enough," or, "I face challenges with courage and grace."
- **Mindfulness Moments:** Pause periodically to observe your thoughts without judgment. Acknowledge them, then let them drift like clouds.
- **The Gratitude Journal:** At the end of each day, write down three things you're grateful for. This will shift your focus from worries to appreciation.

Transformation: These practices reframe Mental Hellfire as a tool for insight, revealing patterns and beliefs that no longer serve us.

2. Physical Awareness: Listening to the Body

Physical Hellfire reminds us that the Body is a vessel for our emotions, stress, and energy. When we ignore it, the fire manifests as pain or fatigue. By listening to the Body, we transform discomfort into a guide.

Daily Practices:

- **Body Scans:** Take five minutes each day to mentally scan your Body, noticing areas of tension or discomfort.
- **Movement Rituals:** Incorporate gentle stretching, yoga, or walking to release stored tension.
- **Nourishment Check:** Before eating, ask yourself, "How does this nourish my body?" Choose foods that energize rather than deplete.

Transformation: These practices turn Physical Hellfire into a reminder to care for and honor the Body, fostering a deeper connection with yourself.

3. Emotional Resilience: Embracing Vulnerability

Emotional Hellfire often stems from suppressed feelings that demand acknowledgment. By allowing ourselves to feel, we release the fire's grip and transform it into healing energy.

Daily Practices:

- **Emotional Check-Ins:** Ask yourself, "What am I feeling right now?" Name the emotion without judgment.
- **Creative Expression:** Art, music, or writing are used to process emotions. Let the fire flow onto the page or canvas.
- **Sacred Tears:** Allow yourself to cry when needed. Tears are a natural release, letting the fire cleanse the soul.

Transformation: These practices turn Emotional Hellfire into a source of strength, teaching us that Vulnerability is not a weakness but a path to authenticity.

4. Spiritual Connection: Finding Purpose in the Flames

Spiritual Hellfire arises when we feel disconnected from meaning or the divine. By cultivating a sense of wonder and gratitude, we transform spiritual crises into opportunities for renewal.

Daily Practices:

- **Sacred Rituals:** Light a candle, meditate, or say a prayer each morning to ground yourself in intention.
- **Moments of Awe:** Take time to marvel at the natural world—a sunrise, a flower, a bird in flight. Let these moments remind you of life's beauty.
- **The Gratitude Walk:** Spend time in nature, thanking the universe for its gifts. With each step, focus on something you appreciate.

Transformation: These practices reignite the spiritual flame, showing us that even in the darkest moments, there is light to be found.

5. Psychic Balance: Harnessing Intuition

Psychic Hellfire can feel overwhelming, especially for those sensitive to energy. By grounding and protecting ourselves, we transform intuitive chaos into clarity.

Daily Practices:

- **Grounding Exercises:** Imagine roots growing from your feet into the earth, anchoring you in stability.
- **Energy Clearing:** Use sage, sound, or visualization to cleanse your energetic field.
- **Intuition Journal:** Record dreams, insights, or synchronicities to understand and trust your intuitive gifts.

Transformation: These practices turn Psychic Hellfire into a source of guidance, helping us navigate life with heightened awareness and trust in our inner wisdom.

The Light of Hellfire: Lessons for Daily Life

By integrating these practices into daily life, we embrace Hellfire as a force of transformation. Its flames, once feared, become a beacon of light, teaching us profound truths:

1. The Fire is a Teacher

Hellfire's challenges reveal what needs attention. The mental critic points to unhealed insecurities. The Body's pain signals neglected care. The heart's grief shows the depth of love. Each flame offers a lesson.

2. Growth is Cyclical

Hellfire is not a one-time experience but a recurring cycle. Each passage through the flames refines us, burning away the old and making way for the new. Embracing this cycle allows us to grow with grace.

3. Wholeness is Found in Integration

The dimensions of Hellfire—mental, physical, emotional, spiritual, and psychic—are interconnected. Healing requires addressing all aspects of the self. We become whole by weaving these lessons into our lives.

Living the Transformation

Imagine Nathan returning to his daily life after his journey through Hellfire. He wakes each morning with gratitude, acknowledging the light within him. He approaches challenges not with fear but with curiosity, seeing them as opportunities to grow. His relationships thrive because he leads with vulnerability and authenticity. Nathan's story reminds us that the fire, when embraced, transforms not only our lives but also the lives of those around us.

The Fire as a Source of Light

Hellfire is not our enemy—it is our ally. Its flames illuminate the parts of ourselves we might otherwise overlook, pushing us toward growth, healing, and connection. By weaving its lessons into our daily lives, we transform the fire from a force of destruction into a light source, creating resilient, authentic, and radiant lives.

WEAVING THE LESSONS OF HELLFIRE INTO DAILY LIFE

Transforming Fire into Light

Introduction: From Chaos to Clarity

The flames of Hellfire are often viewed with dread, their intensity threatening to consume everything in their path. Yet, within these fires lies the seed of transformation. When we resist the fire, it spreads unchecked, leaving destruction. When we lean into its heat, we discover its purpose—not to destroy but to illuminate. By weaving the lessons of Hellfire into our daily lives, we learn to transform chaos into clarity, pain into power, and fear into freedom.

The Framework in Action: Lessons from the Fire

1. Mental Hellfire: Rewriting the Inner Narrative

Reflection:

Mental Hellfire thrives on our stories of inadequacy, failure, and fear. These narratives shape our perceptions and influence every decision we make. To transform Mental Hellfire, we must challenge these stories and create new ones that reflect our inherent worth.

Story: Ella's Inner Critic

Ella was a talented artist, but her mind was her harshest critic. Every brushstroke felt like a test, and every piece of art seemed to fall short of perfection. One evening, overwhelmed by self-doubt, she almost abandoned her dream of exhibiting her work. But a chance encounter with a fellow artist changed everything. "The world needs your perspective," he said. "Even imperfect art tells a story."

Inspired, Ella began reframing her thoughts. She started a journal where she wrote down her fears and then countered them with affirmations. "My work has value," she wrote one evening. "I am enough, just as I am." Over time, the flames of her Mental Hellfire diminished, replaced by the steady warmth of self-acceptance.

Daily Practice:

Pause when self-doubt arises. Ask yourself, "What is the story I'm telling? Is it true?" Reframe negative thoughts with compassionate truths.

2. Physical Hellfire: Listening to the Body's Wisdom

Reflection:

The body speaks in whispers before it shouts. Physical Hellfire often begins as subtle discomfort—a stiff neck, a tired back—but grows when ignored. Transforming this fire requires tuning in and treating the body as an ally rather than a burden.

Story: Mark's Wake-Up Call

Mark had always pushed his body to its limits, priding himself on his endurance. But after years of neglect, his knees began to ache, a constant reminder of the strain he'd ignored. One morning, he collapsed during a run, his body refusing to carry him further.

In recovery, Mark learned to respect his body's boundaries. He incorporated restorative practices like stretching and swimming into his routine. "My body isn't a machine," he realized. "It's a partner." Over time, the physical fire that once consumed him became a gentle guide, reminding him to balance effort with care.

Daily Practice:

Before starting your day, check in with your body for five minutes. Ask, "What do you need today?" Honor the answer, whether it's rest, movement, or nourishment.

3. Emotional Hellfire: The Power of Vulnerability

Reflection:

Emotional Hellfire burns brightest when feelings are suppressed. Grief, anger, and fear demand to be felt and acknowledged. By leaning into vulnerability, we allow the fire to release its hold, transforming pain into healing.

Story: Priya's Tears

Priya had spent years holding back her emotions, believing strength meant silence. After her husband's passing, she tried to move forward without addressing her grief. But one day, while cleaning out his belongings, she found a handwritten letter he'd never sent. The raw emotion in his words broke her open, and for hours, she cried, letting out years of suppressed sorrow.

That evening, Priya realized that her tears weren't a sign of weakness but a release. She began a daily ritual of lighting a candle and writing letters to her husband, expressing her buried emotions. Her vulnerability became her strength, allowing her to reconnect with life.

Daily Practice:

Set aside time daily to reflect on your emotions and express what's in your heart through journaling, art, or conversation.

4. Spiritual Hellfire: Rekindling the Flame of Purpose

Reflection:

Spiritual Hellfire often leaves us questioning our purpose and connection to the divine. It strips away superficial beliefs, inviting us to more profoundly and authentically rediscover faith.

Story: Ahmed's Sunrise

After months of spiritual crisis, Ahmed woke early, drawn outside by an inexplicable pull. He watched as the first rays of sunlight broke over the horizon, painting the sky in hues of gold and pink. At that moment, Ahmed felt an overwhelming sense of peace. The sunrise reminded him that light always returns even after the darkest night.

From then on, Ahmed made it a daily practice to watch the sunrise. It became his sacred ritual, a reminder of life's cycles' renewal and beauty. Through this simple act, he rekindled his faith—not in answers, but in the mystery and wonder of existence.

Daily Practice:

Create a simple ritual that connects you to the divine—a walk in nature, lighting a candle, or spending a moment in silence.

5. Psychic Hellfire: Harnessing Intuition

Reflection:

Psychic Hellfire challenges us to navigate heightened sensitivity and Intuition. Although it can feel overwhelming, it also offers profound guidance when embraced with balance.

Story: Elise's Light

After months of vivid dreams and energetic overload, Elise began to fear her intuitive gifts. But a mentor taught her a grounding practice: Each morning, Elise would imagine herself surrounded by a protective golden light. She visualized the light shielding her from negativity while allowing her to connect with the wisdom of her Intuition.

With practice, Elise learned to trust her insights and use them to help others. Her gifts, once overwhelming, became a source of clarity and purpose.

Daily Practice:

Start your day with a grounding visualization. Imagine roots growing from your feet into the earth and a protective light surrounding you.

The Light of Hellfire: Transforming Daily Life

Integrating these practices into daily routines transforms Hellfire into a source of light and wisdom. Its lessons ripple outward, touching every part of our lives:

1. **Relationships:** Vulnerability deepens connections, allowing for authentic and compassionate interactions.
2. **Work:** Mindfulness and balance prevent burnout, fostering creativity and resilience.
3. **Self-understanding:** Reflecting on Hellfire's lessons reveals the interconnectedness of our struggles and strengths.

Living as the Light

Nathan's story and the stories of Sarah, Mark, Priya, Ahmed, and Elise remind us that Hellfire is not an end but a beginning. Its flames refine us, burning away what no longer serves and revealing our true identity. By weaving its lessons into daily life, we transform from individuals consumed by fire into beacons of light, guiding ourselves and others toward healing, growth, and renewal.

WEAVING ADDITIONAL REFLECTIONS FOR GREATER DEPTH

Attitude and Environment: The Power to Transform Hellfire

Our attitude and environment act as catalysts in transforming Hellfire into Light. While Hellfire burns within us, how we perceive and respond to its flames determines whether it becomes a force of destruction or a source of illumination. By fostering a growth mindset and creating supportive surroundings, we invite the fire to guide us toward renewal, not ruin.

Reflections on Attitude: Shifting Perspective

1. Embracing the Fire as a Teacher

Hellfire often feels like punishment, but what if it's an invitation? Viewing life's challenges as lessons shifts the narrative from victimhood to empowerment.

Reflection:

Nathan's initial resistance to his grief and doubt only deepened his pain. It wasn't until he saw his struggles as an opportunity for growth that he began to heal. This shift in perspective turned his Mental Hellfire into a teacher, showing how his beliefs about success were holding him back.

Daily Practice:

When faced with a challenge, ask, "What is this trying to teach me?" Write down your insights, no matter how small. Over time, this practice fosters gratitude for the lessons hidden in hardship.

2. Choosing Gratitude Over Resentment

Gratitude is a powerful antidote to Hellfire's flames. It doesn't erase pain but reframes it, helping us focus on what remains rather than what is lost.

Reflection:

Priya's grief could have consumed her, but gratitude transformed her pain into purpose. By honoring the love she shared with her husband, she shifted her focus from what she lost to what she cherished.

Daily Practice:

Start or end your day by listing three things you're grateful for. Include even small joys—a kind word, a moment of peace, or a favorite song. Gratitude shifts your mindset, softening the fire's intensity.

3. Cultivating Patience and Self-Compassion

Hellfire tests our patience, pushing us to the edge of our endurance. Cultivating compassion for ourselves during these trials allows us to sit with the fire without being consumed by it.

Reflection:

Sarah's perfectionism fueled her Mental Hellfire, but self-compassion extinguished its flames. By forgiving herself for mistakes and allowing herself to grow, she turned her inner critic into an ally.

Daily Practice:

When self-doubt arises, place your hand over your heart and say, "I'm doing my best, and that is enough." Pair this with deep breaths to calm the mind and body.

Reflections on Environment: Creating Space for Light

1. The Role of Physical Space

Our physical surroundings influence how we experience Hellfire. Cluttered, chaotic spaces often mirror and amplify internal turmoil.

Creating a calm and clear environment helps us gracefully navigate the fire.

Reflection:

When Carlos treated his body carefully, he extended that respect to his surroundings. He cleared his workspace of unnecessary items, creating a sanctuary to focus on healing. This act mirrored the inner clarity he sought.

Daily Practice:

Dedicate weekly time to decluttering a small area of your home or workspace. Choose objects that inspire peace and joy—plants, candles, or meaningful photos—to anchor the space in positivity.

2. Surrounding Yourself with Supportive People

Hellfire isolates us, but the presence of supportive relationships can act as a balm. Surrounding yourself with people who listen, encourage, and challenge you to grow transforms the fire into a shared journey.

Reflection:

Nathan's turning point came when he opened up to Greg. That single act of vulnerability eased his pain and deepened their bond. Nathan discovered that he wasn't alone by inviting others into his fire.

Daily Practice:

Reach out to a trusted friend or family member for a heart-to-heart conversation. Share your struggles and listen to theirs. Authentic connections create a safe space for transformation.

3. Connecting with Nature

Nature is one of the most powerful environments for transformation. The growth, decay, and renewal cycles remind us that fire is a natural part of life—a force that clears the old to make way for the new.

Reflection:

Ahmed's sunrise ritual reconnected him with the divine rhythms of nature. The rising sun symbolized hope each morning, teaching him that light always follows darkness.

Daily Practice:

Spend time outdoors each day, even if only for a few minutes. Notice the textures of leaves, the sound of the wind, or the sun's warmth. Let nature's resilience inspire your own.

Transforming Hellfire: A Shift in Energy

1. Turning Struggle into Service

One of the most profound ways to transform Hellfire is to channel its energy into helping others. Sharing our stories and supporting those in their fires creates a ripple effect of light.

Reflection:

Once overwhelmed by her Psychic Hellfire, Elise found purpose in using her gifts to guide others. By embracing her sensitivity, she transformed her life and became a beacon for those around her.

Daily Practice:

Ask yourself, "How can my experience help someone else?" Whether offering advice, volunteering, or simply listening, acts of service redirect Hellfire's energy into healing.

2. Finding Meaning in Pain

Hellfire often strips us of the comforts and illusions we cling to, leaving us bare. In this emptiness lies the opportunity to create new meaning and purpose.

Reflection:

After finishing his father's clock, Nathan realized that his journey through Hellfire wasn't just about personal growth—it was about authentically honoring his father's legacy. This realization transformed his pain into a source of pride and purpose.

Daily Practice:

When reflecting on a challenging experience, ask, "What meaning can I create from this?" Write down the lessons or values that emerged from the fire.

The Integration of Attitude and Environment

Attitude and environment are not separate—they are deeply intertwined. A positive mindset shapes our surroundings, just as a supportive environment nurtures a resilient attitude. Together, they create a cycle of transformation, where Hellfire becomes not an obstacle but an ally.

Reflection Exercise: The Interconnected Web

1. Choose a challenge you're currently facing.
2. Reflect on your attitude toward this challenge. Are you resisting or leaning into the fire?
3. Assess your environment. Does it support or hinder your transformation?
4. Write down one small change you can make to shift your attitude or environment toward light.

Becoming the Light

Hellfire is a universal force, touching every life in deeply personal yet profoundly connected ways. By shifting our attitude and cultivating environments that nurture growth, we transform its flames into a guiding light. This light illuminates our path and serves as a beacon for others, reminding us all that within every fire lies the potential for renewal, resilience, and radiant strength.

More profound Examples: How Attitudes and Environments Transform Hellfire

1. **Relationships:** The Fire of Disconnection

Relationships often bring both light and heat. Hellfire ignites when unspoken emotions, unmet expectations, or unresolved conflicts build tension. Transforming the fire requires vulnerability, active listening, and a willingness to create a supportive environment.

Story: Anna and Liam

Anna and Liam had been married for ten years, but their connection had frayed over time. Anna felt unappreciated, and Liam felt misunderstood. Arguments sparked over minor issues, leaving both feeling burned by resentment.

One evening, after a particularly heated argument, Anna changed her approach. Instead of criticizing Liam for not helping around the house, she wrote him a heartfelt letter explaining how his support made her feel loved and valued. To her surprise, Liam responded by opening up about his insecurities—he hadn't realized how his behavior affected her.

The letter became a turning point. They established weekly “check-ins" to share feelings and needs openly. Their relationship shifted as they replaced blame with understanding, transforming the fire of disconnection into a flame of rekindled love.

Key Takeaway:

Transforming Hellfire requires creating an environment of trust and open communication in relationships. Vulnerability becomes the bridge that turns conflict into connection.

Daily Practice:

Set aside 10 minutes daily to ask a loved one, "How are you feeling?" Listen without interrupting or offering solutions. Create a safe space for authenticity.

2. **Careers:** The Fire of Burnout

Hellfire in the workplace often manifests as burnout—a combination of Mental, Physical, and Emotional Hellfire caused by overwork, lack of recognition, or misaligned goals. Transforming this fire requires shifting attitudes about success and creating environments that support balance.

Story: Maya's Reassessment

Maya was a marketing executive who worked 12-hour days, fueled by the belief that her worth was tied to her productivity. When her health began to decline—frequent migraines, constant fatigue—she realized she was trapped in a cycle of burnout.

Her turning point came when a mentor asked, "What do you want your work to stand for?" The question forced Maya to confront her motivations. She realized she wanted to create meaningful campaigns, not just hit targets. With her mentor's guidance, Maya set boundaries: no emails after 6 p.m., daily walks, and delegating non-essential tasks.

Over time, Maya rediscovered her passion for her work. She transformed burnout into purpose by redefining success and creating a healthier work environment.

Key Takeaway:

In careers, transforming Hellfire requires aligning daily tasks with deeper values and creating systems prioritizing well-being.

Daily Practice:

Each morning, write down three tasks that align with your long-term goals. End your workday by reflecting on your accomplishments and setting boundaries for tomorrow.

3. **Parenting:** The Fire of Overwhelm

Parenting often brings Hellfire in the form of Mental and Emotional strain. The constant demands of caregiving can lead to feelings of inadequacy and exhaustion. Transforming this fire requires shifting expectations and creating environments that foster joy and connection.

Story: Rachel's Reset

Rachel, a single mother of two, often felt like she was failing. Her days were a whirlwind of work, school pickups, and endless chores. Her breaking point came when her daughter said, “You're always too busy to play with me."

That night, Rachel reflected on her priorities. She realized she was trying to do everything ideally instead of focusing on what mattered most—her children's happiness. She made minor changes: dedicating 20 minutes each evening to playtime, involving her kids in cooking, and letting go of minor messes.

These shifts created a lighter atmosphere at home. Rachel felt less overwhelmed, and her children became more cooperative and joyful. The fire of overwhelm transformed into a warm hearth of love and togetherness.

Key Takeaway:

In parenting, transforming Hellfire requires embracing imperfection and finding joy in the small moments.

Daily Practice:

At the end of each day, ask your child, "What was the best part of today?" Share your answer, too, fostering connection and gratitude.

How Attitudes and Environments Shape Hellfire Across Areas of Life

1. **Attitude:** The Internal Flame

Your mindset shapes how you perceive and respond to Hellfire. A fixed mindset sees challenges as threats, while a growth mindset views them as opportunities for learning.

Key Shift:

Replace "Why is this happening to me?" with "What can I learn from this?"

Example: Ahmed's crisis of faith transformed when he began to see unanswered prayers not as abandonment but as an invitation to trust life's mysteries.

Daily Practice:

When faced with a challenge, write down three hidden lessons or opportunities.

2. **Environment:** The External Flame

Your surroundings influence how Hellfire manifests and how you navigate it—a supportive environment—whether physical, social, or emotional—buffers against the fire's intensity.

Key Shift:

Cultivate spaces that reflect your values and nurture your well-being.

Example: Elise's intuitive overwhelm eased when she created a peaceful home environment with grounding elements like plants, soft lighting, and quiet spaces.

Daily Practice:

Take one weekly Action to improve your environment, such as decluttering, adding natural elements, or setting boundaries with negative influences.

Reflection Exercise: Transforming Your Hellfire

1. **Identify the Fire:**

Which dimension of Hellfire—mental, physical, emotional, spiritual, or psychic—is most prominent in your current life?

Example: "I feel burned out from constant deadlines at work."

2. **Examine Your Attitude:**

What beliefs or narratives are fueling this fire?

Example: "I need to work late every night to prove my worth."

3. **Assess Your Environment:**

How is your environment contributing to the fire?

Example: "My workspace is cluttered, and I'm surrounded by colleagues who glorify overwork."

4. **Take Action:**

What small changes in attitude or environment could transform this fire into light?

Example: "I'll remind myself that my worth isn't tied to my productivity and create a clutter-free, calming workspace."

5. **Transforming Fire into Light**

Hellfire is not an isolated phenomenon—it touches every corner of our lives, from our relationships and careers to our inner world. By shifting our attitudes and curating supportive environments, we harness its energy as a catalyst for growth. In doing so, we become active participants in our transformation, turning the fire that once threatened to consume us into a guiding light.

Practices for Fostering Resilience and Growth

Resilience and growth are cultivated through intentional practices that empower us to navigate life's challenges and harness the transformative energy of Hellfire. These practices span life's mental, emotional, physical, spiritual, and social dimensions, offering tools to build strength, adaptability, and purpose.

MENTAL RESILIENCE: STRENGTHENING THE MIND

1. The Power of Reframing What It Is: Reframing involves shifting your perspective on challenges and turning obstacles into opportunities for growth.

How It Fosters Resilience: It rewires the brain to focus on solutions rather than problems.

Practice:

- When faced with a setback, write down the challenge in one column and potential lessons or opportunities in another.
- **Example:** Losing a job might open the door to pursuing a more fulfilling career.

2. The Focused Five

What It Is: A daily practice identifying five key priorities or intentions.

How It Fosters Resilience: Helps reduce overwhelm by focusing energy on what truly matters.

Practice:

- Each morning, write down five priorities for the day. Keep the list realistic and meaningful.
- **Example:** "1. Complete project proposal. 2. Call Mom. 3. Walk for 20 minutes. 4. Practice gratitude. 5. Prepare dinner mindfully."

Emotional Resilience: Honoring the Heart

3. Emotional Check-Ins

What It Is: A simple, daily reflection on your emotional state.

How It Fosters Resilience: Encourages emotional awareness and prevents suppressed feelings from building into Emotional Hellfire.

Practice:

- Set an alarm three times daily (morning, midday, evening). When it goes off, pause and ask yourself: "What am I feeling right now?" Please write it down.
- **Example:** "Morning: Calm. Midday: Frustrated. Evening: Grateful."

4. The Gratitude Letter

What It Is: Write a heartfelt letter to someone who has positively impacted your life.

How It Fosters Resilience: Strengthens emotional bonds and shifts focus to appreciation.

Practice:

- Write a letter of gratitude to a friend, family member, or mentor. If possible, deliver it.
- **Example:** "Dear Sarah, your support during my health scare meant the world to me…"

Physical Resilience: Nurturing the Body

5. The Body Compass

What It Is: Daily tuning into your body's needs.

How It Fosters Resilience: Prevents Physical Hellfire by addressing discomfort and restoring balance.

Practice:

- Each morning, ask: "What does my body need today?" Choose one action that supports this need.
- **Example:** "My shoulders feel tense. I'll take a 5-minute break after every hour of work."

6. Restorative Rhythms

What It Is: Aligning your daily routine with natural cycles, such as circadian rhythms.

How It Fosters Resilience: Enhances energy, focus, and Recovery.

Practice:

- Set consistent sleep and wake times. In the morning, expose yourself to natural light and limit screen time before bed.
- **Example:** Aim for 7-8 hours of sleep and a tech-free hour before bedtime.

Spiritual Resilience: Connecting to Purpose

7. The Anchor Ritual

What It Is: A grounding ritual reconnecting you with your purpose.

How It Fosters Resilience: Provides a sense of stability amidst uncertainty.

Practice:

- Choose a simple daily ritual that reflects your values, such as lighting a candle, praying, or meditating.
- **Example:** "Each morning, I light a candle and reflect on one thing I'm grateful for."

8. Moments of Awe

What It Is: Seeking experiences that evoke wonder and expand your perspective.

How It Fosters Resilience: Reminds you of the beauty and interconnectedness of life.

Practice:

- Spend time in nature, watch a sunset, or listen to moving music. Reflect on how it makes you feel.
- **Example:** "Today, I'll take 10 minutes to watch the clouds and marvel at their patterns."

Social Resilience: Building Supportive Connections

9. The Circle of Support

What It Is: Identifying and nurturing relationships that uplift and inspire you.

How It Fosters Resilience: Strengthens your ability to face challenges with a sense of community.

Practice:

- List three people you trust to support you emotionally. Schedule regular check-ins with them.
- **Example:** "Call my sister every Friday to share how our weeks went."

10. The Energy Audit

What It Is: Assessing the energy you gain or lose from relationships and adjusting.

How It Fosters Resilience: Protects you from draining connections and fosters positive ones.

Practice:

- Reflect on interactions from the day. Identify relationships that energize or deplete you and adjust your boundaries accordingly.
- **Example:** "Spending time with Jen lifts me; I'll plan more coffee dates with her."

Integration Across Life Dimensions

To maximize resilience and growth, combine these practices across dimensions, tailoring them to specific areas of your life:

Relationships:

- Use the Gratitude Letter to strengthen bonds.
- Practice The Energy Audit to set boundaries and prioritize supportive connections.

Career:

- Implement The Focused Five to stay aligned with meaningful goals.
- Use Restorative Rhythms to enhance productivity and prevent burnout.

Parenting:

- Practice Emotional Check-Ins to model emotional awareness for your children.
- Create an Anchor Ritual with your family, such as a daily moment of gratitude.

REFLECTION: BUILDING RESILIENCE DAILY

1. **Morning Intention:**
   Begin each day with a grounding practice. Ask yourself: "What do I want to focus on today?"
   Example: "Today, I'll approach challenges with curiosity."
2. **Midday Check-In:**
   Pause at lunchtime to assess your energy and mindset. Adjust as needed.
   Example: "I feel drained. I'll take a 10-minute walk to recharge."
3. **Evening Reflection:**
   End the day by reflecting on what you learned from the challenges.
   Example: "I realized that asking for help made my workload lighter and strengthened my connection with my team."

Resilience as a Lifelong Practice

Resilience isn't about avoiding Hellfire but learning to walk through it with grace. By integrating these practices into your daily life, you cultivate the strength to face challenges, the adaptability to grow from them, and the wisdom to transform fire into light.

Facing the Flames

Life's greatest trials often feel like unrelenting flames—overwhelming, consuming, and devastating. Yet, just as fire refines gold and births the Phoenix, these challenges are also opportunities for transformation. This book invites you to step into your Hellfire, not to be destroyed by it, but to emerge from it stronger, clearer, and more radiant than ever before.

The Symbolism of Fire – A Universal Teacher

Fire is a paradoxical force: it destroys yet purifies, terrifies yet illuminates. Across cultures and philosophies, fire has been revered as both a destructive and transformative element. To understand our Hellfire, we must first embrace its duality.

Mythological Symbols

- **The Phoenix**: Its cyclical renewal from ashes teaches us that destruction is the seed of new life.
- **Hindu Agni**: The fire god represents the sanctifying power of challenges, consuming impurities, and connecting humanity to the divine.
- **Alchemy's Flame**: Transformation occurs through the burning away of what no longer serves, unveiling enlightenment.

Psychological Insights

- **Carl Jung's Shadow Work**: Fire as a symbol of integrating the darker aspects of ourselves.
- **Joseph Campbell's Hero's Journey**: The trials of fire mold us into more complete versions of ourselves.

Reflection: What does fire symbolize in your life? How has it shaped you?

The Cycles of Hellfire – Embracing Transformation

Transformation is not a single event but an ongoing cycle. Each phase of Hellfire challenges us to grow, adapt, and emerge renewed.

Phases of the Cycle

1. **Ignition**: The catalyst—a loss, betrayal, or crisis—that sparks transformation.
2. **Descent**: Facing intense challenges that consume outdated beliefs.
3. **Surrender**: Letting go of resistance to make space for growth.
4. **Integration**: Weaving lessons into a stronger sense of self.
5. **Renewal**: Emerging, transformed, and ready for the next cycle.

Practical Exercise

- Reflect on a past challenge and identify its phases. Where are you in your current cycle?

Turning Challenges into Growth

Resilience transforms Hellfire into a force for personal and collective growth. This chapter examines how resilience applies to real-life scenarios, helping readers relate and grow.

Scenario 1: The Single Parent Balancing Work and Family

Maria's resilience shifted her focus from guilt to gratitude, using rituals and affirmations to reclaim her peace.

Scenario 2: The Professional Facing Career Burnout

James rediscovered his purpose by redefining Success, creating space for Recovery, and contributing through mentorship.

Scenario 3: The Young Adult Navigating Uncertainty

Emma's journey through comparison and fear led her to clarity and connection through reflection, vulnerability, and visioning.

Collective Hellfire – Rising Together

Hellfire is not just personal—it is shared. Humanity faces collective challenges, from pandemics to climate change, that test our resilience and unity.

Examples of Collective Renewal

- Communities rebuilding after natural disasters.
- Social justice movements transforming pain into progress.
- Global efforts to address environmental crises.

Call to Action

- **Be a Light in Your Community**: Share your lessons and inspire those around you.
- **Advocate for Change**: Use your voice and actions to contribute to a better world.
- **Inspire Unity**: Focus on connection over division.

THE HELLFIRE TOOLKIT

Navigating Hellfire is a deeply personal journey, but you don't have to face it unarmed. Just as every fire requires specific tools to contain and control it, your inner flames can be tempered with practices that engage your mind, body, and soul. This chapter equips you with actionable strategies to navigate Hellfire across five key dimensions: mental, emotional, physical, spiritual, and psychic.

Each tool is designed to help you find clarity, build resilience, and emerge from the flames stronger than ever. While these practices are universally beneficial, the key is to adapt them to your unique challenges, making your Hellfire Toolkit a reflection of your personal journey.

1. Mental Resilience Tools

Your mind is where Hellfire often begins, sparked by self-doubt, overthinking, or negative beliefs. Mental resilience is about rewiring these patterns, replacing fear with clarity, and transforming limiting thoughts into empowering ones.

Journaling for Reflection

Journaling provides a safe space to explore your thoughts and emotions, free from judgment. It helps you identify patterns, clarify your feelings, and release mental clutter.

Practice: Begin each day with a simple prompt: *"What is my greatest challenge today, and how can I approach it with resilience?"* End the day by reflecting on lessons learned.

Example: If you feel overwhelmed at work, use journaling to unpack your stress, identify actionable solutions, and reframe the situation.

Reframing Negative Thoughts

Reframing shifts your perspective from fear or failure to opportunity and growth.

Practice: When a negative thought arises, write it down and counter it with a positive reframe. For example, "I'll never succeed" becomes "Every step I take brings me closer to success."

Example: When facing rejection, reframe it as redirection toward something better suited to your growth.

Mindfulness Practices

Mindfulness anchors you in the present moment, preventing your mind from spiraling into worst-case scenarios.

Practice: Set aside five minutes daily for mindful breathing. Inhale for four counts, hold for four counts and exhale for four counts, focusing solely on your breath.

Example: When you feel overwhelmed, pause and use this technique to regain calm and clarity.

2. Emotional Resilience Tools

Hellfire can ignite intense emotions—fear, anger, sadness—that feel overwhelming. Emotional resilience involves honoring and processing these feelings, allowing them to guide rather than consume you.

Gratitude Exercises

Gratitude shifts your focus from what's missing to what's present and meaningful.

Practice: Each night, write down three things you're grateful for. They can be as simple as a kind word from a friend or the warmth of sunlight on your skin.

Example: During a period of loss, gratitude for small joys can remind you that light persists, even in darkness.

Emotional Release Rituals

Unprocessed emotions can fuel your Hellfire. Releasing them is a crucial step toward healing.

Practice: Create a safe space to express your emotions physically. This could be screaming into a pillow, punching a heavy bag, or crying freely.

Example: After a breakup, a guided visualization where you release anger into a firepit can help you let go of the pain.

Connection Practices

Emotions are easier to process when shared. Vulnerability creates bonds that sustain you through the flames.

Practice: Schedule weekly check-ins with a trusted friend or family member where you both share your struggles and victories.

Example: When dealing with workplace stress, talking openly with a mentor can provide perspective and relief.

3. Physical Resilience Tools

Hellfire often manifests physically as tension, fatigue, or illness. Building physical resilience helps you regain strength, ground yourself, and maintain vitality.

Grounding Techniques

Grounding reconnects you to the present moment and your physical body, anchoring you amid emotional storms.

Practice: Walk barefoot on grass, sand, or earth while focusing on the sensations beneath your feet. Alternatively, hold an object like a stone or crystal and focus on its texture and weight.

Example: Use grounding after a stressful meeting to reset your energy and regain focus.

Movement for Release

Physical activity helps burn off excess stress hormones, releasing tension and boosting mood.

Practice: Choose an activity that resonates with you—yoga for calm, running for exhilaration, or dancing for joy.

Example: After a heated argument, a brisk walk or a spontaneous dance session can help you process and release pent-up emotions.

Self-Care Routines

Caring for your body strengthens your resilience to external pressures.

Practice: Establish routines that include nourishing meals, adequate hydration, and restful sleep. Treat self-care as non-negotiable.

Example: When overwhelmed, prioritize a soothing evening ritual like a warm bath, herbal tea, and calming music.

4. Spiritual Resilience Tools

Hellfire challenges your sense of purpose and connection to something greater. Spiritual resilience helps you find meaning, anchor in your values, and trust in the journey.

Morning Intentions

Setting an intention at the start of your day aligns your actions with your values.

Practice: Light a candle or take a deep breath and set an intention like "Today, I will approach challenges with grace."

Example: On a difficult day, this practice helps you stay focused on who you want to be, regardless of circumstances.

Meditation for Clarity

Meditation quiets the noise of the mind, creating space for inner guidance to emerge.

Practice: Begin with five minutes of silent meditation, focusing on your breath or a mantra like "I am resilient."

Example: During a major life decision, meditation can help you access the wisdom within.

Sacred Rituals

Rituals provide a sense of sacredness and structure, reminding you of your connection to the divine or universal energy.

Practice: Create a personal ritual, like journaling under the moonlight or offering gratitude before meals.

Example: A weekly gratitude ritual can help you stay grounded in what truly matters during chaotic times.

5. Psychic Resilience Tools

The psychic dimension relates to your energy field—how you protect and sustain your inner power amid external challenges.

Energy-Clearing Practices

Energy-clearing removes stagnant or negative energy, leaving you feeling refreshed and empowered.

Practice: Burn sage or palo santo, or visualize a white light washing over you, clearing away negativity.

Example: After a draining interaction, a quick energy-clearing ritual helps you reclaim your equilibrium.

Visualization for Protection

Visualization strengthens your boundaries and shields your energy.

Practice: Imagine yourself surrounded by a protective bubble of light, allowing love and positivity to flow in while keeping negativity out.

Example: Use this visualization before entering potentially stressful situations, like a family gathering or a high-stakes meeting.

Boundary-Setting

Clear boundaries protect your energy from unnecessary depletion.

Practice: Identify one area where your boundaries feel weak and create a simple action plan to reinforce them. For example, say "no" to commitments that drain you.

Example: When a colleague frequently offloads their stress onto you, setting a boundary ensures your energy isn't consumed by their flames.

Building Your Personalized Hellfire Toolkit

Not every tool will resonate with everyone, and that's okay. The key to building your personalized Hellfire Toolkit is experimentation and adaptation. Consider these steps:

Assess Your Needs: Reflect on which dimension—mental, emotional, physical, spiritual, or psychic—feels most impacted by your current Hellfire.

Start Small: Choose one practice from that dimension to try for a week.

Evaluate: Notice how it affects your resilience, mood, and overall energy.

Expand: Gradually incorporate practices from other dimensions, creating a balanced toolkit.

Closing Reflection

The Hellfire Toolkit is not just a collection of practices—it's a lifeline, a sanctuary, and a source of empowerment. Each tool you use brings you closer to the truth that the flames are not here to destroy you but to refine you. By engaging with these practices, you honor your journey and build the resilience to navigate any fire that life may bring. The fire within you is your greatest ally—use these tools to harness it.

The Light Within – Embracing Your Inner Fire

Every Hellfire you face reflects your fears, illusions, and truths. The flame within you, however, remains steady, guiding you through life's trials.

Practical Exercises

Daily Reflection: Ask yourself, "What did today's challenges teach me?"

Symbolic Rituals: Light a candle as a reminder of your resilience.

Affirmations: Repeat, "The fire within me is stronger than the flames around me."

Illuminating the Path for Others

Transformation is not just personal—it's communal. By sharing your light, you inspire others to rise from their flames.

How to Share Your Light

Tell Your Story: Vulnerability inspires others.

Offer Support: Be a compassionate listener.

Lead by Example: Show resilience through your actions.

Preparing for Future Fires – Facing Tomorrow with Strength and Grace

Life's challenges are not isolated events; they are part of an ongoing, cyclical process of growth and renewal. Just as seasons return and tides rise and fall, the flames of Hellfire reappear throughout our lives. But each time they come, they do so not to destroy but to refine. This chapter equips you with the tools and mindset to face future fires with courage, readiness, and a promise of success. By learning to anticipate and navigate challenges, you will not only endure them but thrive because of them.

UNDERSTANDING THE NATURE OF FUTURE FIRES

Future Hellfires can take many forms—unexpected losses, changes in relationships, career upheavals, or even internal crises of identity and purpose. While we cannot always predict their arrival, we can prepare ourselves to meet them with strength. Preparation does not eliminate the flames, but it ensures that we face them with clarity and purpose, transforming their heat into light.

The Promise of Success in Facing Challenges

Success in the face of future Hellfires is not measured by avoiding pain or struggle but by how we adapt, grow, and emerge from the flames. With the right tools and perspective, every fire can be an opportunity to deepen your resilience, refine your purpose, and strengthen your connection to yourself and others.

What Success Looks Like:

Clarity: Understanding the root of the challenge and what it is asking you to release or embrace.

Resilience: Facing the flames without being consumed by them, knowing you have the tools to navigate through.

Growth: Emerging from the experience with new insights, strengths, and a sense of empowerment.

Practical Tools for Navigating Future Fires

The following tools are designed to equip you with the awareness, stability, and support needed to approach future challenges. By practicing these regularly, you'll build a foundation of readiness that ensures you can weather any storm and rise stronger.

1. Self-Awareness: Recognizing the Early Signs

Self-awareness is your first line of defense. By recognizing the early signs of a Hellfire, you can respond proactively rather than reactively. This awareness requires tuning into your emotional, mental, and physical state to identify shifts that may signal an impending challenge.

Signs to Look For:

Emotional turbulence, such as heightened anxiety, irritability, or sadness.

Mental patterns of overthinking, self-doubt, or a sense of stagnation.

Physical symptoms like fatigue, tension, or disrupted sleep.

Building Self-Awareness:

Daily Check-Ins: Take five minutes each day to ask yourself:

How am I feeling emotionally, mentally, and physically?

What has shifted recently in my life or within myself?

Is there anything I'm avoiding or resisting?

Track Patterns: Keep a journal to note recurring emotions or experiences. Over time, you'll notice patterns that can help you anticipate challenges.

Promise of Success: With heightened self-awareness, you can identify the spark of a Hellfire before it becomes overwhelming, allowing you to approach it calmly and with intention.

2. Grounding Rituals: Staying Centered During Trials

When a fire begins to rage, staying grounded is essential. Grounding rituals anchor you in the present moment, preventing the flames of fear or panic from consuming you. These practices create a sense of stability, helping you navigate challenges with clarity and control.

Key Grounding Techniques:

Breathwork: Slow, intentional breathing calms your nervous system and focuses your mind.

Practice: Inhale for four counts, hold for four counts, and exhale for four counts. Repeat until you feel centered.

Physical Grounding: Connect with the earth through touch or movement.

Practice: Walk barefoot on grass, hold a grounding object like a stone, or practice gentle yoga stretches.

Visualization: Imagine roots growing from your feet into the earth, anchoring you firmly as the flames swirl around you.

Creating a Grounding Ritual:

Choose one or two techniques that resonate with you and practice them regularly, even when life feels calm. This builds muscle memory, making it easier to access these tools during a challenge.

Promise of Success: By mastering grounding rituals, you'll remain steady and clear-headed even in the face of life's most intense fires, allowing you to make thoughtful decisions and preserve your energy.

3. Community Support: Building a Network of Resilience

No one is meant to face Hellfire alone. Community support is a powerful tool for navigating challenges, offering strength, perspective, and encouragement when your own reserves feel depleted. The key is to cultivate relationships and networks that can sustain you during difficult times.

Why Community Matters:

Shared experiences reduce feelings of isolation and remind you that you're not alone.

Others can provide insights, resources, or encouragement that you might not find on your own.

Mutual support fosters resilience, as giving and receiving strength creates a ripple effect.

Building Your Support Network:

Identify Trusted Allies: These can be friends, family, mentors, or community groups. Look for individuals who are empathetic, reliable, and nonjudgmental.

Establish Regular Check-Ins: Schedule weekly or monthly conversations with your support network to share challenges and victories.

Create a Resilience Group: Form a small group of like-minded individuals committed to supporting each other's growth. This could be a book club, spiritual group, or online community.

Reaching Out During Hellfire:

Don't hesitate to ask for help when you need it. Be honest about your struggles and clear about how others can support you.

Practice vulnerability, knowing that opening up is a sign of strength, not weakness.

Promise of Success: With a strong support network, you'll face every fire with a sense of solidarity, knowing you have people to lean on and grow with.

Putting It All Together: A Plan for Readiness

Success in navigating future fires lies in integrating these tools into your daily life, making resilience a habit rather than a reaction. Here's how to start:

Create Your Toolkit: Identify which tools resonate most with you—self-awareness practices, grounding rituals, or community support—and commit to using them regularly.

Practice in Calm Periods: Don't wait for the fire to arrive. Practice these tools during periods of calm, so they become second nature when challenges arise.

Reflect and Refine: After each Hellfire, reflect on what worked and what didn't. Adjust your toolkit to better meet your needs for the next cycle.

The Promise of a Resilient Future

The flames of future Hellfires may flicker on the horizon, but they no longer need to bring fear. With self-awareness, grounding rituals, and the support of a strong community, you are equipped not only to face these fires but to thrive because of them. Each challenge becomes a stepping stone, a chance to deepen your resilience, refine your purpose, and emerge stronger.

As you prepare for future fires, remember this: the flames are not here to destroy you but to transform you. You carry within you the strength to navigate any challenge and the promise of success that each cycle of Hellfire brings. When the fire comes again, you will face it with courage, ready to rise anew.

A Vision for Humanity – Rising Together

When individuals transform their Hellfires into light, they contribute to a brighter world. Together, we can rise from our collective flames, creating a humanity rooted in resilience, unity, and hope.

BECOMING THE LIGHT

The fire you faced did not destroy you—it revealed you. It illuminated your truth, your resilience, and your purpose. Now, it's time to carry that light forward, living as a beacon of hope for others.

Blessing for the Journey

"May your light burn bright, even in the fiercest flames. May you walk boldly through every fire, knowing that within you lies the power to transform. And may your journey inspire others to find their own light, until the world itself is illuminated by our collective brilliance."

The Cycles of Hellfire – Embracing Transformation

Transformation is not a singular event or a straight path. It unfolds in cycles, mirroring the rhythms of nature: the rising and setting of the sun, the changing seasons, and the eternal ebb and flow of life. Hellfire, with its intensity and power, is no different. Each phase of this cycle challenges us to grow, adapt, and emerge renewed, forging resilience and clarity through the flames.

To embrace transformation is to understand these cycles—not as moments to fear but as opportunities to refine and rediscover yourself. By identifying and navigating each phase, you can move through Hellfire with grace, confidence, and the knowledge that every fire leads to renewal.

Phases of the Hellfire Cycle

1. Ignition: The Catalyst

The cycle begins with a spark—an unexpected event or realization that sets the fire alight. Ignition is the moment when life as you knew it shifts. It could be a loss, betrayal, crisis, or even a moment of profound self-awareness. While this phase is often marked by pain and upheaval, it also carries the seed of transformation.

Signs of Ignition:

- Sudden emotional upheaval, such as shock or grief.
- Feeling as though your life has been upended.
- A growing awareness that change is unavoidable.

Progress in Ignition: Recognizing that this disruption, though painful, holds the potential for growth is the first step toward transformation. Progress in this phase comes from accepting the spark rather than resisting it.

Example: When Sarah lost her job unexpectedly, she initially felt devastated. But as she sat with the reality of her situation, she realized this loss was a chance to reimagine her career path—a path she had long felt unfulfilled by.

2. Descent: Facing the Flames

After the spark ignites, the fire spreads, consuming outdated beliefs, habits, and patterns. The descent is the most challenging phase, as it requires you to confront the depths of your pain, fears, and limitations. It's here that Hellfire feels most intense, but it's also where the greatest breakthroughs occur.

Signs of Descent:

- Intense emotional struggles such as fear, anger, or despair.
- A sense of loss as old identities, routines, or relationships dissolve.
- Feeling "in the dark," unsure of the way forward.

Progress in Descent: Growth in this phase comes from allowing yourself to feel and process the intensity of your emotions rather than avoiding them. Progress means acknowledging the fire as a teacher, even if its lessons are painful.

Example: When David went through a divorce, he felt consumed by regret and anger. But as he journaled daily, he began uncovering patterns in his relationships that he hadn't addressed before. This awareness, though painful, became the foundation for his eventual healing.

3. Surrender: Letting Go

As the fire continues to burn, there comes a moment when resistance becomes futile. Surrender is not about giving up; it's about releasing control and making space for growth. It's a moment of profound humility and acceptance, where you allow the fire to do its work without clinging to what was.

Signs of Surrender:

- A growing sense of peace amidst the chaos.
- Acceptance of what cannot be changed.
- A willingness to let go of outdated identities, beliefs, or attachments.

Progress in Surrender: In this phase, progress looks like releasing the "shoulds" and "what-ifs" that keep you stuck. By surrendering, you create space for new possibilities to emerge.

Example: Maria, who had always defined herself by her career, found herself at a crossroads when her company shut down. After weeks of fighting against reality, she finally embraced the idea that this was an opportunity to explore passions she had long ignored. Surrender opened the door to rediscovery.

4. Integration: Weaving the Lessons

Once the flames have burned away what no longer serves you, the process of integration begins. Here, you take the lessons learned during the descent and surrender phases and weave them into a stronger, more authentic sense of self. Integration is where transformation becomes tangible—where the new version of you begins to take shape.

Signs of Integration:

- A deeper understanding of the lessons the Hellfire revealed.
- Clarity about your values, priorities, and goals.
- A renewed sense of self that feels more aligned and authentic.

Progress in Integration: Progress means applying what you've learned to your daily life. It might involve setting boundaries, nurturing new habits, or embracing a new perspective. This phase requires patience, as transformation is a gradual process.

Example: After months of introspection following her divorce, Emily began prioritizing self-care and healthier relationships. The insights she gained during her descent became the foundation for a more fulfilling life.

5. Renewal: Emerging Transformed

Renewal is the culmination of the Hellfire cycle—a phase marked by new beginnings, strength, and clarity. It's the moment you step out of the flames, not as the person you were, but as the person you were meant to become. Renewal doesn't mean life will be free from challenges, but it does mean you now carry the tools, resilience, and wisdom to face them.

Signs of Renewal:

- A sense of empowerment and readiness for the next chapter.
- Gratitude for the journey, even its most painful moments.

- A renewed commitment to living authentically and purposefully.

Progress in Renewal: In this phase, success lies in stepping confidently into the new chapter of your life, trusting that the Hellfire has prepared you for what's ahead.

Example: After months of grieving her father's passing, Anna felt a deep sense of peace and connection to his memory. She channeled her grief into creating a community art project in his honor, turning her pain into purpose.

Practical Exercise: Mapping Your Hellfire Cycle

Take a moment to reflect on a past challenge or the one you're currently facing. Identify where you are in the cycle and journal about the following prompts:

Ignition: What event or realization sparked this cycle? How did it disrupt your life?

Descent: What beliefs, emotions, or patterns have you had to confront? How have you faced them so far?

Surrender: What are you holding onto that needs to be released? How can you create space for growth?

Integration: What lessons have you learned? How can you apply them to your life moving forward?

Renewal: How has this experience transformed you? What strengths or insights have emerged?

THE POWER OF EMBRACING THE CYCLE

RISING THROUGH THE FLAMES

Life is an ever-turning wheel of growth, challenge, and renewal. The Hellfire cycle reflects this eternal rhythm—a transformative process that refines and reshapes us at every turn. To embrace this cycle is to embrace life itself, with all its intensity, beauty, and complexity. The flames may test you, but they also reveal the strength and brilliance within you, lighting a path toward the person you are destined to become.

The Transformative Nature of the Cycle

Transformation is rarely linear. It is not a straight road but a spiraling journey, one that revisits familiar struggles with new perspectives and deeper lessons. Each phase of the Hellfire cycle challenges you to meet life's trials not with resistance but with intentionality and courage. The journey is not about rushing through the flames to escape discomfort; it is about moving through them deliberately, allowing their heat to refine you.

Insight: The Alchemy of Fire

Fire transforms everything it touches. It turns wood to ash, ore to gold, and raw emotions into wisdom. In the same way, your Hellfire burns away what no longer serves you—outdated beliefs, fears, and attachments—leaving behind the essence of your truest self. By embracing the fire, you become your own alchemist, turning pain into purpose and struggle into strength.

Stories of Transformation: Walking Through the Flames

Transformation is not a theoretical concept; it is a lived experience. Here are stories of individuals who embraced the Hellfire cycle and emerged transformed:

1. A Mother's Journey: From Loss to Legacy

After losing her teenage son in a tragic accident, Rachel found herself engulfed in grief. For months, she resisted the pain, drowning in questions of "Why?" and "What if?" Her Ignition phase was raw and overwhelming. But one day, she stumbled upon her son's unfinished journal, where he had written about his dream of helping homeless youth.

The fire shifted. Rachel entered the surrender phase, releasing her resistance and choosing to honor her son's dream. She started a foundation to support at-risk teenagers. Through Integration, Rachel wove her grief into her purpose, and in Renewal, she found healing—not because the pain disappeared but because it became a source of meaning.

Lesson: Rachel's journey shows that the flames of loss can reveal a path to profound purpose. The fire that initially feels like destruction often clears the way for something greater.

2. A Professional's Awakening: From Burnout to Balance

James was a high-achieving executive whose life revolved around work. His Ignition came when a stress-induced health scare forced him to confront his unsustainable pace. In the phase of Descent, James faced uncomfortable truths about his need for external validation and his neglect of personal well-being.

Surrender came when he let go of the belief that his worth was tied to productivity. He began to prioritize self-care and realigned his career with his values. Through Integration, James developed new habits—leaving work on time, practicing mindfulness, and mentoring young professionals. Renewal came in the form of a more balanced, fulfilling life, where success was defined by impact rather than exhaustion.

Lesson: James's story illustrates that burnout is not the end but a signal for transformation. By embracing the fire, he rebuilt his life with intention and clarity.

3. The Phoenix Rises: A Personal Transformation

Anna had always been afraid of confrontation, avoiding difficult conversations at all costs. Her Ignition came when a close friendship fell apart due to unresolved tensions. In Descent, Anna faced her fear of conflict and the belief that her voice didn't matter. She realized that avoiding confrontation was costing her meaningful relationships.

Surrender came when Anna decided to step into discomfort and have the difficult conversations she'd been avoiding. She sought therapy, practiced assertiveness, and slowly rebuilt her self-confidence. Integration followed as she began using her voice to set boundaries and strengthen connections. In Renewal, Anna found a new sense of empowerment—she was no longer afraid to speak her truth.

Lesson: Anna's journey reminds us that the flames of fear often conceal the strength we need to grow. By walking through the fire, she discovered her power and transformed her relationships.

Why Embracing the Cycle Matters

1. The Cycle Is Inevitable

Hellfire is not a one-time event. Throughout life, the flames will return, each time revealing new layers of growth. Recognizing this cyclical nature allows you to approach challenges with acceptance rather than resistance, knowing that every fire is part of a greater process.

2. The Fire Refines, Not Destroys

In the midst of a Hellfire, it's easy to feel consumed. But the fire's purpose is not destruction—it is refinement. Like gold in a crucible, you are being purified, your essence revealed through the heat of transformation.

3. Renewal Awaits

The final phase of the cycle, Renewal, is your proof that the journey is worth it. Every flame you walk through prepares you for the next chapter of your life, one marked by greater clarity, strength, and purpose.

Practical Wisdom: Embracing the Flames

To fully embrace the Hellfire cycle, you must engage with it actively and intentionally. Here are profound ways to navigate each phase:

1. In Ignition: Acknowledge the Spark

Practice: When a challenge arises, name it. Say aloud or write down, *"This is my fire. It is here to teach me something."*

Insight: Acknowledgment is the first step in transforming fear into curiosity.

2. In Descent: Face the Heat

Practice: Sit with your emotions without judgment. Use journaling or therapy to explore what the fire is asking you to release.

Insight: The flames often illuminate truths you've been avoiding. Facing them is where growth begins.

3. In Surrender: Let Go

Practice: Identify one belief or attachment that the fire is urging you to release. Consciously choose to let it go, perhaps through a ritual like writing it on paper and burning it.

Insight: Surrender is not weakness; it is the ultimate act of courage and trust in the process.

4. In Integration: Weave the Lessons

Practice: Reflect on what the fire has taught you and identify one way to apply that lesson to your daily life.

Insight: Transformation is not about forgetting the fire—it's about carrying its wisdom with you.

5. In Renewal: Step Forward

Practice: Celebrate your growth, whether through a personal ritual, a creative project or simply sharing your journey with someone else.

Insight: Renewal is not just the end of the cycle; it is the beginning of the next one, with you now stronger and wiser.

The Promise of the Cycle

Transformation isn't easy, but it is always worth it. Each Hellfire you face holds a promise: the promise of growth, clarity, and renewal. When you embrace the cycle, you reclaim your power to rise, not as the person you were, but as the person you were destined to become.

A Final Reflection: The Eternal Dance of Flames and Light

The flames will come—it is the nature of life. They will arrive unbidden, their intensity igniting fear, discomfort, and often pain. But just as surely as the flames rise, so too will the light follow. For every fire that touches your life, there is an equal and opposite force within you: the light of resilience, wisdom, and boundless potential. It is this light that transforms the fire from a force of destruction into one of creation, turning ashes into fertile ground and wounds into wisdom.

You have walked through the fire before, haven't you? You've felt its searing heat, the weight of its demands, and the silence that follows in its wake. And yet, here you are—not diminished, but changed. Not broken, but reassembled into a version of yourself that is wiser, stronger, and more attuned to the rhythm of life.

The Truth of the Fire

The truth is this: Hellfire is not your enemy. It is your teacher, your catalyst, and your companion in growth. Each fire carries a message, asking you to let go of what no longer serves you and embrace the essence of who you are becoming. The fire burns not to harm but to purify, stripping away illusions, fears, and outdated beliefs, leaving behind the unshakable truth of your inner self.

Fire as Transformation

Think of the ancient Phoenix, reborn from its ashes, each cycle of destruction a prelude to renewal. The Phoenix is not consumed by its fire; it is refined by it. In the same way, every fire you face is a doorway—not an ending but a beginning. And when you walk through that doorway, you emerge not as you were, but as you were destined to be.

The Light That Follows

The flames may feel all-encompassing, but they are never eternal. What lasts is the light—the clarity and strength that emerge when the fire subsides. This light is not something external; it is a reflection of the brilliance within you. It is your resilience, your courage, your capacity to rise again and again.

Carrying the Light Forward

Each time you rise from the ashes, you carry with you the gifts of the fire:

Wisdom: The deep, unshakable knowing that you have faced the impossible and survived.

Strength: The quiet power of resilience that grows with every trial.

Compassion: The empathy born from understanding pain and using it to uplift others.

A JOURNEY THROUGH THE FLAMES

Reflect on your own journey. Can you see the fires that once seemed insurmountable, the moments when the flames licked at your heels, and the smoke obscured your vision? Can you recall the times when you doubted your ability to rise? And yet, you did.

A Story of Renewal

Consider Sarah, who lost her home in a wildfire. In the weeks that followed, she grieved not just the loss of her possessions but the life she had built within those walls. But as she sifted through the ashes, Sarah found an unexpected clarity. Freed from the weight of material attachment, she chose to rebuild her life with intention, focusing on relationships, purpose, and experiences over things. The fire had taken much, but it had also given her the light of renewal—a life truer to her essence than the one she had lost.

The Promise of Rising

Every time the flames comes, they bring with them the promise of transformation. This is not to diminish the pain or challenges they bring but to remind you that within every trial lies the seed of something new. The fire may feel all-consuming, but it is also temporary. What remains is the person you become—the one who has faced the flames and risen, carrying the fire's transformative gift forward into a life of greater purpose, resilience, and light.

A New Perspective

To live with this understanding is to live with courage. It is to see the flames not as something to fear but as something to embrace, knowing that they are part of your evolution. Each fire clears the way for new growth, and each light that follows illuminates your path with greater clarity.

A Blessing for the Journey

As you move forward, know this: The flames may come again, but they will never find you unprepared. With every lesson learned, every truth embraced, and every renewal completed, you become stronger, more radiant, and more attuned to the rhythm of life.

A Final Blessing

"May you face the flames with courage, knowing that within you lies the power to transform. May you walk through the fire with grace, trusting in the light that will follow. And may you rise from the ashes, not as the person you were, but as the person you were meant to be—stronger, wiser, and ablaze with purpose."

The Eternal Promise

The journey through fire is the journey of life itself—a dance of destruction and creation, fear and courage, darkness and light. Each cycle refines you further, shaping you into a vessel of resilience and a beacon of hope. And so, when the flames come again, remember: You are not walking into the fire alone or unprepared. You are walking into the next chapter of your transformation, carrying within you the eternal promise of the light that will follow.

This Is Your Sacred Path

Your journey is unlike any other, woven with the threads of your soul's unique purpose. It is a sacred path, one illuminated by moments of grace and shadowed by trials meant to refine and deepen your essence. Every step, no matter how painful or joyous, is imbued with meaning, shaping you into the person you are destined to become.

To walk this journey is to honor the divine spark within you—a light that burns brighter with every challenge you embrace, every truth you uncover, and every transformation you undergo. The road is not always easy, but it is always sacred, for it is your soul's evolution.

The Divine Rhythm of Life

Life moves in cycles, each one a sacred dance of creation and destruction, of endings and beginnings. The trials you face are not random—they are the whispers of the universe, calling you to awaken, to shed the old, and to step into the fullness of your being. Every challenge is a divine invitation to align more closely with your truth and purpose.

Even the flames, those moments of intense struggle, are holy in their purpose. They strip away illusions and falsehoods, revealing the core of who you are. To walk through fire is not to be burned but to be consecrated—to emerge with a soul that is clearer, lighter, and more attuned to the eternal.

The Guidance of the Sacred Flame

The sacred flame within you is your constant guide. It is the whisper of your soul, the pulse of divine love, and the eternal connection to something greater than yourself. This flame cannot be extinguished, not even by life's most intense trials. It is your essence, your truth, and your connection to the infinite.

As you journey forward, let this inner flame be your compass. Trust it to light your way through the darkest nights and to illuminate the lessons hidden within every shadow. The path may twist and turn, but the flame remains steady, reminding you of your inherent divinity and your ability to rise.

The Promise of the Eternal

Your journey is not bound by time or space—it is eternal. Every step you take echoes across the fabric of existence, weaving a story of transformation and transcendence. The challenges you face are not detours; they are milestones of spiritual awakening, guiding you closer to the divine essence within and around you.

There is no moment on this path that is wasted, no trial that does not hold a sacred purpose. Every experience, every tear, every triumph is a part of the tapestry of your becoming. To walk this path is to align with the flow of the universe and to trust that you are exactly where you are meant to be.

A Sacred Benediction

May your journey be blessed with the wisdom to see the sacred in every step. May you find peace in knowing that you are never alone, for the divine walks beside you, within you, and before you. May you trust the flames to refine and not destroy, and may you rise from every trial more luminous than before.

The Spiritual Truth

This is your sacred journey. It is guided by divine hands, fueled by an eternal flame, and marked by profound transformation. Though the path may challenge you, it is designed to awaken the deepest truths of your soul. To walk this journey is to embrace the infinite—to become the light you were always meant to be. And that, above all, is worth everything.

Thank you for choosing to read this book; your time and curiosity mean the world to me.

www.ingramcontent.com/pod-product-compliance
Lightning Source LLC
LaVergne TN
LVHW010926110826
845149LV00013B/2494